PRAISE FOR *SAY GRACE*

"*Say Grace* is a powerful and moving reminder that people are the heart and soul of our industry, and that taking care of each other is our first—and most sacred—responsibility. Enormous credit is due Steve Palmer for generously sharing his story and dedicating his remarkable career to helping others in the true spirit of hospitality."

DANNY MEYER*; founder and CEO, Union Square Hospitality Group; author,* Setting the Table

"We're at a watershed moment in the hospitality industry, a time when the conversation about addiction and mental health crises is finally coming to the fore thanks to the courage of leaders like Steve Palmer. A call to action and a love letter to restaurant people, *Say Grace* will empower those who work in the business to take care of themselves and one another as much as they do their customers."

HUNTER LEWIS*, editor-in-chief,* Food & Wine

"*Say Grace* is a just-as-I-am spiritual story of a gifted leader who has the courage and grace to share his struggles so that others may miss the battle scars of coming back home to the soul of humans and hospitality: taking care of others."

CLIFF OXFORD*; founder, Oxford Center for Entrepreneurs and STI Knowledge, an INC-13 company; author,* Lambs to Leaders *and* Know Grow Exit

"Steve Palmer saves lives. I couldn't begin to count the number of people I've guided toward him and Ben's Friends when they were in a moment of crisis, because I know he'll be standing there with open arms and a way to safety. His kind, steadfast example will anchor the restaurant industry for decades to come."

KAT KINSMAN; *senior editor,* Food & Wine; *author,* Hi, Anxiety: Life with a Bad Case of Nerves

"Restaurateur and community leader Steve Palmer offers a raw and unflinching account of his battles with drug and alcohol addiction, not to say, "Hey, look at me," but, "Hey, there's hope." I applaud his courage, his honesty, and his ongoing mission to help others struggling with addiction."

DARCY SHANKLAND, *editor-in-chief,* Charleston Magazine

"*Say Grace* is a celebration of life, a celebration of an industry and the people in it. Steve's amazing journey is so inspiring, and his love for the business of hospitality resonates with anyone who has ever worked or dined in his restaurants."

MICKEY BAKST, *restaurateur and cofounder of Ben's Friends*

SAY GRACE

Steve **Palmer**

FOREWORD BY JOHN T. EDGE

SAYGRACE

How the Restaurant Business *Saved My Life*

Published by ForbesBooks, Charleston, South Carolina.
Member of Advantage Media Group.

ForbesBooks is a registered trademark, and the ForbesBooks colophon is a trademark of Forbes Media, LLC.

Printed in the United States of America.

10 9 8 7 6 5 4 3 2 1

ISBN: 978-1-94663-396-5
LCCN: 2019915224

Cover design by George Stevens.
Layout design by Carly Blake.

This publication is designed to provide accurate and authoritative information in regard to the subject matter covered. It is sold with the understanding that the publisher is not engaged in rendering legal, accounting, or other professional services. If legal advice or other expert assistance is required, the services of a competent professional person should be sought.

Advantage Media Group is proud to be a part of the Tree Neutral® program. Tree Neutral offsets the number of trees consumed in the production and printing of this book by taking proactive steps such as planting trees in direct proportion to the number of trees used to print books. To learn more about Tree Neutral, please visit **www.treeneutral.com**.

Since 1917, the Forbes mission has remained constant. Global Champions of Entrepreneurial Capitalism. ForbesBooks exists to further that aim by bringing the Stories, Passion, and Knowledge of top thought leaders to the forefront. ForbesBooks brings you The Best in Business. To be considered for publication, please visit **www.forbesbooks.com**.

This book is dedicated to the women and men of the restaurant business who accepted me where I was, loved me when I couldn't love myself, and gave a sense of purpose and meaning to my life that I could have never imagined. I will never have enough words to express my gratitude. From the bottom of my heart, thank you.

CONTENTS

Foreword

THE DUALITY OF THE RESTAURANT INDUSTRY

"We are an incredibly giving industry. We care for others ...
We serve guests, but we don't serve each other. We give
back to the community while abandoning our own."

Those hard sentences come late in this good book. What comes before that is hard, too. You hurt for the young man you get to know. For the twelve-year-old who drunkenly wandered his suburban Atlanta neighborhood. For the fourteen-year-old who, in the age of Nancy Reagan's intolerant "Just Say No" campaign, suffered through a horrifically abusive treatment program. For the homeless sixteen-year-old who fed himself with food he stole from convenience stores.

Read Steve's book and you better understand the promise and peril of the restaurant industry. You marvel at how the restaurant business saved his life. And now, thanks to this book, you recognize how the restaurant industry can save itself.

In his twenties, Steve found unconditional love and acceptance, working in bars and restaurants in and around Atlanta and Charleston.

"They didn't care who you knew or where you were from," Steve writes, sounding a familiar refrain among industry lifers. "If you showed up for your shifts and worked hard, you were part of the family."

By the time he was in his thirties, Steve was drinking handles of vodka and doing bumps of cocaine in the walk-in. Car wrecks, arrests, and relationships piled up. Lies big and tragic and small and demeaning took tolls. When Steve tried to quit drinking on his own, "turtles emerged from the drywall and flew around the room in circles before disappearing into nothing."

Steve was earning a partner's share in a luxe Charleston restaurant that set national standards for food and service. But his life was a mess. Two colleagues intervened. They forced him into treatment. That's the duality of the restaurant world, Steve writes. The same industry that had fed his addictions also fueled his recovery.

Steve makes clear the stakes when people who work in this industry fail to get the help they need. He makes it hurt. He makes it personal. And—here's the spoiler—he does something to fix the problem. To meet the needs of members of his restaurant family struggling with substance abuse or addiction, Steve and a friend cofounded Ben's Friends in 2016.

Named for Ben Murray, a chef friend of Steve's who committed suicide after a long fight with alcoholism, the organization is now expanding beyond its base in the South, working to normalize recovery for addicted restaurant industry employees. The aim is to end the stigma. The promise is to resolve the duality. Steve speaks directly to his colleagues when he writes here, "We need to care for each other the way we care for our guests."

JOHN T. EDGE, *director of the Southern Foodways Alliance at the University of Mississippi, host of* TrueSouth *on SEC/ESPN, author of* The Potlikker Papers

A WORD FROM
THE AUTHOR

This will be the only book I ever write. I am a restaurateur, not a professional writer, and I have only one story to tell—this one. It is both a celebration and an examination of the hospitality industry as viewed from the perspective of a recovering addict and alcoholic.

The hospitality industry operates under a perplexing contradiction. We are an industry of caring individuals whose job it is to care for others—but we are failing to care for our own. The industry enabled my addiction so readily, so completely, that I nearly drank myself to death on the job. But that same industry consists of wonderful, caring people who helped bring me back from the brink. I achieved sobriety in an industry steeped in alcohol and drugs, but it was only with the help of others.

Historically, the hospitality industry has been inhospitable to sobriety. From "bad boy" celebrity chefs living the sex, drugs, and rock 'n' roll lifestyle to the bravado and rationalization of getting sloshed every night at the end of our shifts, the industry has long glorified and glamorized alcohol and drug use.

The results have been neither glorious nor glamorous.

People are dying. Lives are being destroyed. The time for change is long overdue.

Thankfully, the industry has finally gotten the wake-up call. For the first time, we are talking openly about the addiction and mental health crises that plague our industry. This is a watershed moment. It's the time to speak openly about what is happening and how we can all help.

This is why I founded Ben's Friends with Mickey Bakst, a nonprofit organization dedicated to helping industry people get the aid they need to stay sober in a wet industry. It's also why I wrote this book. My story is specific to me, but it is far from unique. The hospitality industry is full of people struggling with addiction and mental health issues—and they don't know where to turn. They don't know that help is out there. They don't know that many of their coworkers are also struggling or already sober. It's time to open up, speak out, and effect real change.

It's time to open up, speak out, and effect real change.

I owe my life to sobriety and my sobriety to the people who stepped forward to intervene and offer care. I had thought it impossible to be sober in this industry. Kind people showed me otherwise. With their help, I got sober and stayed in the industry to help make it better.

A better future is possible for the industry and everyone in it. We all need to put out a hand and lift each other up. We need to care for each other the way we care for our guests. We need to speak freely and honestly about the problems in our industry.

This book is my attempt to do just that. I found community and grace in the hospitality industry, despite its problems, and believe that others can as well. Together, we can do better.

Chapter 1

AT THE END OF
THE BOTTLE

THE LAST STRAW

September 30, 2001

The sun was just threatening the horizon as I staggered up to our apartment in the little blue house at 33 Society Street in downtown Charleston. The hint of orange low in the sky told me it was about five or six o'clock in the morning, which meant that I had broken my promise not to stay out all night. After closing down the Peninsula Grill, where I was the general manager, I had called my wife to let her know that some of us were going out to the bar.

"Don't stay out all night."

"I won't," I promised.

I worked the doorknob carefully with my keys, cradling them to avoid the jingle, and crept through the apartment. My wife looked asleep in bed. I climbed into the other side of the bed and pulled the covers over me, careful not to wake her. I didn't want her seeing my state. I was strung out on cocaine but also drunk enough to pass out as soon as my head hit the pillow.

It was almost afternoon when I woke. My wife was already up. I had been out so hard from the alcohol that I hadn't heard her pack up her things and load them into the car. This I would find out only later.

She was waiting for me in the living room. I could tell we were about to have a serious talk. It turned out to be a short one.

"I'm leaving," she said. "As long as I stay here, you're going to stay sick."

I had made and broken the same promises every single night, every single day, for years.

There wasn't much else to say. We both knew the truth. It wasn't just about having stayed out all night. It wasn't just about the liquor and the drugs. It was that I had made and broken the same promises every single night, every single day, for years. The promises to come home. The promises not to drink till drunk. The promises not to call the coke dealer. Broken promise upon broken promise—all of them compounding. Every single time, the promise was broken.

Every time, she had looked the other way. Every time, she'd cleaned up my messes for me. She had come to see herself as an enabler. She realized she was doing me no favors. She was only making matters worse, and she could see that now. So she had to leave, for her own sake, and also for mine.

And so she left. I was thirty-two years old. We had been married for about a year and a half and had been dating much longer. We met working in the service industry. She was waiting tables. I was working the bar. We actually used to go out drinking together more. I had always envied the way she could go out drinking after work and close out her tab after a pint or two. She could drink like a normal person. When it became clearer and clearer that I could not do the same, spending time together in that way became harder, which was part of why I stayed out so late. Being around each other was harder and harder.

So the separation came as no surprise. In fact, as sad as it sounds, it came as a *relief.* I felt sad that she was going. I also felt guilty, knowing that this was all my fault. But the overriding emotion was just a sense of relief that no one was going to be around to hold me responsible. I could now stay out drinking without offering excuses. Hell, I could stay *in* and drink without having to make excuses. There would be no more worrying about the optics of the bottles piling up in the bin. I wouldn't need to sneak shots while she was in the bathroom. Without my wife there to watch my fall, I wouldn't have to face criticism.

The person with whom I had walked down the aisle and exchanged eternal vows was leaving forever, and I was actually relieved. That was how addiction had twisted my mind. I was celebrating my own divorce—not because I wanted a divorce but because divorce would make it easier to feed my addiction.

LEFT TO MY OWN DEVICES ...

October 2001

With my wife gone, there was no one at home to hold me accountable, and my drinking did escalate even further. I was already reaching for the bottle as her car pulled away. I took a few slugs to get my head straight and got ready for work. I kept drinking at work and got totally hammered afterward. The next day the same: rinse and repeat forever.

This wasn't categorically different from before. I had been drinking all day, every day, for years. I could put away a half gallon to a gallon of vodka a day. At the restaurant, I would sneak shots of Grand Marnier ("bartenders' heroin," as we called it in the industry) from inventory. I could drink a whole bottle by myself over the course of a night and then go out for cocktails and still buy a bottle of liquor for the road. The only big change was that there was now reason to go even harder.

I was self-isolating more than before my wife left. With the apartment to myself, I spent less time at the bar. After closing down the restaurant, I would usually give the coke dealer a call and pick up an eight ball or so and a handle of vodka. I spent most nights drinking alone. This wasn't normal for me. I have always been a social person, but drinking at home was cheaper and easier.

Without my wife at the apartment, I started leaving a bottle of vodka out on the nightstand so I could take a slug first thing in the morning. I carried the bottle with me to the shower and sipped at it to get straight. My hands would shake in the mornings. Without a couple of eye-openers, my whole body would start to shake. I needed drinks first thing just to do simple things like brushing my teeth. I didn't have the coordination without the alcohol. There were times I would shave two handed, one hand holding the razor and the second hand steadying the first, just to keep from cutting myself.

Drinking like this was not fun. No one wakes up in the morning and slugs some vodka to get the party started. You wake up and start drinking just to get through the day. Without drinking in the morning and throughout the day, I couldn't make it through work.

I had to sneak shots of Grand Marnier from the liquor cabinet and walk down the block for a few beers during break just to get through the workday.

People were starting to take notice. The chef at the restaurant pulled me aside to say he was concerned. This was one of my drinking buddies. We used to stay out all night together, knocking back shots. If he was concerned, I really had a problem.

"Your wife left you, and you're hurting. I get it," he said. He encouraged me to refocus and pour my energy into the restaurant, as it could be my salvation. "*This* is your home now. You don't have to worry about your marriage anymore. It's over. Reset your priorities. Don't let this destroy you. It's an opportunity."

The owner of the restaurant, Hank Holiday, also confronted me but with more of a tough love approach. He issued a warning. My behavior was reflecting poorly on the restaurant. The Peninsula Grill was an upscale establishment with a reputation to protect. Charleston wasn't that large of a town, and the restaurant scene wasn't very big. People knew each other, and it didn't look good when the GM of the restaurant was out all night at the bars, getting trashed and strung out.

"You're the ambassador of this restaurant," he said. "People can see what's going on. You need to get your act together."

He was right. I had always taken a misguided pride in being able to "handle" my liquor. I was six foot five and weighed in at 250 pounds, most of it muscle and bone. I could toss back obscene amounts of alcohol without passing out, but that tough-guy veneer was starting to crack. Earlier that month, I passed out in a bar for the first time. It was the local food-and-bev hangout spot, which meant that the story made its way around the industry. I couldn't walk. Several friends had to load me into a cab and send me home.

5

I don't remember getting into bed, though I do remember waking up with a pounding headache and calling the coke dealer first thing.

I didn't *want* to buy drugs. I didn't *want* to keep drinking. What I wanted was to get sober. But the inconvenient truth was that I just couldn't. Sobriety wasn't in my power. I was lost and alone—so lost and alone that I couldn't get my life together, much less get sober. I wasn't capable of sober living.

For a long time, I pretended that sobriety wasn't necessary. I had convinced myself that it was possible to run a restaurant doing $5 million annually while taking shots and snorting lines in my office every day. But people *were* noticing. Even one of the wine reps commented on my condition. As the GM, I was also the wine buyer for the restaurant. I would see her only a few times a month, sometimes a few times a year, and even she could see the changes in me.

She came to my house one night to tell me she was worried. The knock at the door startled me. I was even more startled to see this person I barely knew standing in the doorway. She asked to come in. I said yes. We talked for a little while about my drinking and my separation. She didn't shame me. She wasn't there to yell. She was just really worried for me and wanted to be there to listen. It was a kind gesture that didn't feel earned. I was being a total screwup. I didn't deserve empathy. But here was this person I hardly knew, offering her ear and telling me she was worried about me.

When she left, I sat down alone at the kitchen table and started to cry. I knew that if even a casual work acquaintance could tell that things weren't right, they must have been getting really bad. I didn't know how much longer I could hold things together. My life felt wholly out of my control. I was living week to week despite a decent salary. Making rent and bills was harder on my own, especially since so much of my money went into buying cocaine and alcohol. More money wasn't going to solve the problem either—it would only have made things worse. Every extra dime was spent feeding my addictions. I was helpless. My despair and loneliness were so all-consuming that making changes seemed impossible. Being better wasn't in my wheelhouse.

The only thing that kept me going was the alcohol and drugs, the very same things that were creating all of my problems. I was drinking from the moment I rolled out of bed until I passed out at the end of the night. More money meant more alcohol and drugs. And more alcohol and drugs meant a deeper addiction. This is all obvious to someone who isn't an addict, but when you are locked deep into an addiction, you can't see a mile down the road. You can barely see what's right in front of your face.

THREE DAYS OF SOBRIETY

November 2001

Things went on this way for about a month before it all became too unmanageable. I woke up one day and decided enough was enough—I wasn't going to drink that day.

My morning shakes got worse as the day progressed. They started in my hands and moved throughout my whole body. I could hear my teeth chattering. By the next day, things were so bad that I had to lie down in the middle of my living room floor to keep from falling over. My head felt electrified. I was sweating like crazy. I was starting to hallucinate. Shimmering green turtles emerged from the drywall and flew around the room in circles before disappearing into nothing. They looked like holograms, but they were convincingly real.

Though my brain felt broken, I was still surprisingly lucid

throughout this whole ordeal. I remember thinking that as terrible as this felt, it probably wasn't going to be enough to keep me sober. This wasn't my first time trying to quit drinking. I had been through rehab several times. Sometimes I would try to go a day without drinking. I always ended up going back to the bottle. I didn't see any reason to believe that this time would be any different. This wasn't just despair, though I was despairing. There was no way to quit drinking unless someone plucked me up and put me somewhere where it was physically impossible to get alcohol.

Despite being raised Methodist and believing in some abstract notion of God, I was not particularly religious. But in that moment, I started bargaining with God, since bargaining with myself hadn't worked. I was speaking to Him as if he were there in the room, listening to me as I shook on the floor.

> *"God, unless you put me someplace where I can't get alcohol, I'm going to die."*

"God, unless you put me someplace where I can't get alcohol, I'm going to die," I said aloud. "You have to put me somewhere else."

I knew in that moment that the war I had been fighting was lost. Alcohol had won, and there was nothing I could do—not on my own. In the recovery community, people talk about powerlessness over addiction. This was something a little different. I wasn't quite there yet. The recovery community believes that you have to surrender yourself to a higher power in order to stop drinking. I didn't believe that *anything* could stop me from drinking. Nothing short of abandonment on a desert island was going to keep me from drinking.

Until that moment, I had held on to a vague notion of *someday* getting clean and sober. This was a comforting notion that I used to rationalize taking shots at work or doing blow in the bathroom. But that pretense had lifted. I believed that I was hopeless. I would never overcome my addiction. There was nothing to be done in the long run. Maybe I wouldn't drink today; maybe I wouldn't drink tomorrow or the next day. But someday, eventually, I would have a drink, and then another, and another. It felt like there was no getting around this inconvenient truth. I was thirty-two years old and had spent most of my life intoxicated. Short of being locked up forever, I was going to die.

INTERVENTION

November 1, 2001

Despite these realities, I managed not to drink a single drop for three days straight. This was the longest I had gone without alcohol in at least a decade. I also went without cocaine, pot, or anything else.

Eventually, the worst of the withdrawal symptoms started to subside. The hallucinations and shaking were as bad as it got. I later realized how lucky this was. I was ignorant to how dangerous alcohol withdrawal can be. Thankfully, I never had a seizure or went into delirium tremens despite quitting cold turkey after more than a decade of continuous heavy drinking. No one should do what I did. I could have died alone in my apartment.

Somehow I managed to go in to work throughout all of this. I had no option. The owner had already put me on notice. So I did what I had to do and went in to work. My hands were shaking. My clothes stayed soaked with sweat no matter how often I swapped out shirts. I probably looked half crazed. The second and third day, I was still seeing and hearing things that weren't there.

These symptoms didn't go unnoticed. The owner of the restaurant, Hank Holiday, called me into his office. The chef was there too. The looks on their faces told me that they meant business.

"You have a choice to make, and you're going to make it right now," Hank said. "There's a bed waiting for you in rehab. Either you go home now and pack your bag, or you can start cleaning out your office."

I tried bargaining. It had been three days since I had a drink. Three days! They weren't swayed by this fact. Like me, they had doubts that I could *stay* sober, especially at work, where alcohol was always around. They were right—there was nothing I wanted more in that moment than a drink.

"Can I have a moment to think about it?" I asked, wanting to go down the street for a double pour of vodka.

The chef shook his head no. He knew exactly what I had in mind. He'd been there at the bar the night I passed out. "We care about you," he said, knowingly.

"But we aren't going to watch you kill yourself," Hank said. "So which is it going to be?"

I wanted to run and hide. My lizard brain was screaming at me to tell them to get fucked and then storm out of the room. But my heart wasn't in it. I was tired. I was sick. As they say in the recovery community, I was sick and tired of being sick and tired. Still believing in my own inevitable doom, I didn't really think rehab would work. I had already been twice before. But nothing else was working either. Moderation had failed. Making promises to myself had failed. Trying to stick to drinking only on weekends or just smoking pot had failed. I had tried everything, and nothing had worked. Maybe this wouldn't work either, but what was there to lose? Staying sober seemed impossible, but I just didn't have it in me to fight. I didn't even have it in me to run. I was completely broken. I just gave up.

"Okay," I said. "I'll go. I'll pack my bags."

Much later, I would look back on that day and see it as an answered prayer. I had asked to be put somewhere where I couldn't get alcohol. Less than seventy-two hours later, I had people offering to check me into just such a place, unwilling to take no for an answer.

I literally could have said no. I could have taken door number two and packed up my office. It wasn't that I thought rehab would work. I had been there—and here—many times before. I was running out of second chances. I did not have any left. Door number two was going to lead to death.

Chapter 2

A TROUBLED CHILDHOOD

MOURNING

1970s

T he natural tendency of addicts is to blame other people and outside circumstances for their addictions. I don't want to do that here. We all make our own choices in life, and we are ultimately responsible for our own actions.

However, we are also, at least partially, products of our environment. Multiple studies have established a link between trauma and addiction problems. I was probably destined to be an alcoholic from my first sip, but there are reasons why some addicts fall into active addiction earlier and stay there longer.

A series of traumas in my childhood and teenage years played an undeniable role in putting me on the path toward serious, active addiction. I started drinking and using at a very young age. This was definitely the result of a difficult childhood.

My biological mother put me up for adoption. She was only twenty-two years old when she gave birth to me. She wasn't married or partnered. My biological father split when she told him about the pregnancy.

Despite this situation, the early years of my life were fairly normal. My parents adopted me as an infant as well as my older sister. We look nothing alike. I have dark hair and olive skin. Kym is redheaded and fair skinned. Our father was a doctor, our mother a nurse. They provided us a good home in the Atlanta suburbs.

I idolized my father. He was accomplished, kind, caring, and joyous. I couldn't have asked for a better father. He was generous with praise and always supportive. We also had a lot in common. We were both athletes. He played tennis. I played soccer and basketball. I was tall from a young age and excelled at sports. My father came to all of my games, no matter what, for as long as he was able.

My passion was sports. My grades were also good. In the first grade, I tested into a special track for gifted students. I was popular and made friends easily. My life was good in those early years of childhood.

And then my dad got sick. He had been living with diabetes since he was sixteen but managed the disease well. He was active and healthy. As a doctor, he knew how to take care of himself. His health was good despite needing insulin to survive. That all changed when I was about six years old. His kidneys started failing. He lost the ability to walk and went blind. Watching him deteriorate was traumatizing. My hero was crumbling before my eyes. If he wasn't safe, nothing was safe. My sense of safety and well-being was shattered instantly. I was left scared and confused. He quickly went from being able and strong to bedbound in a hospital bed in the living room. He only left the house twice a week, for dialysis.

Nothing seemed to help. He just kept getting sicker. In 1978, a kidney transplant offered a glimmer of hope. Shortly after the transplant, he was back on his feet again. His eyesight came back partially. However, within three months, his body had rejected the transplant, and he was sick again. We had been given a small glimmer of hope only to have it snatched away. A year later, he was dead.

The day he died is etched forever into my memory. It was October 30, 1979. I was ten years old. A neighbor picked Kym and me up from school.

"Your father's very sick today," she said. The pitying tone of her voice told me all I needed to know.

I was heartbroken to lose my father, but in a way his loss was expected. We had watched him deteriorate slowly. His body had been failing before my eyes. In a way, his death was a release for him and a relief for us. Death meant he was no longer struggling, no longer disappointed. Death meant that the pain and the daily indignities of chronic illness were at an end. I remember telling my mom, "Dad is playing tennis in heaven again." I needed to believe that he was okay. Imagining him in heaven was some comfort.

What was more traumatizing than my father's death, for which I was mentally prepared, was having my grandfather diagnosed with lung cancer a mere three months later. My father had declined slowly, but my grandfather went quickly. He was diagnosed with lung cancer in December. We put him in the ground the following September, almost exactly a year after my father, his son, had died. His funeral was on my eleventh birthday.

This was very hard for me. I idolized my grandfather as much as my own father. My grandfather was very much a man of the silent generation. He'd enlisted in the navy and fought against the Japanese in the South Pacific during World War II. In college, he played for the Georgia Bulldogs and had actually taken me to my first Bulldogs game in 1973. He was a war hero and a larger-than-life figure in my mind. But, like many men of his generation, he drank martinis in the evening and smoked Camel unfiltered cigarettes all day long. These would ultimately be the things that killed him.

The loss of my grandfather hit me hard. I used to spend weekends at my grandparents' house, a place of laughter and joy. I loved and respected him as much as my own dad. He had assumed a father-figure role after the decline of my dad's health prevented him from fulfilling that role. My dad used to come to my games on crutches and then in a wheelchair until it became too hard to come at all. My grandfather still came.

Now, they were both gone. Over the course of a single year, I had lost both of my idols. As kids do, I blamed myself. I felt cursed.

It didn't make sense that everyone was dying. The only thing that made sense was that it was something wrong with me.

I remember a teacher saying, "First your dad and now your grandfather? God, Steve. Who is going to die next?" I'm sure she meant well, but this encapsulated my worst fears and greatest doubts about the world. It didn't make sense that everyone was dying. The only thing that made sense was that it was something wrong with me. I was the common thread. Part of me did wonder who would die next.

After the funerals, people filed in and out of the house to pay respects. Someone, either a neighbor or extended family member, told me I had to be the "man of the family" now and needed to take care of my mom and sister. I was eleven and still in elementary school. How could I be the man of the house? I didn't even understand what it meant to be the man of the house any more than I understood why everyone I loved kept dying.

FIRST SIPS

1980

I started drinking shortly after my grandfather passed. My parents weren't big drinkers, but they did keep the wet bar stocked. My first drink was a can of Black Label, a beer originated in Canada, swiped from the refrigerator. At the tender age of eleven, I thought the beer tasted bitter and strangely foamy in my mouth, but I liked the way it warmed my insides and made the edges of my vision soft and blurry. I liked how it numbed the pain and allowed me to breathe a little easier.

After that first beer, I started sneaking booze from the liquor cabinet while my mom was away at work. The house was littered with my dad's old tennis-ball cans. I would empty out the balls and fill the can up with liquor. This made it easy to carry liquor around the neighborhood without being noticed or stopped. I mostly drank alone in the woods near my house. I had no conception of ice or mixers. I just drank straight liquor out of the tennis-ball cans. The first few times, I drank far too much. I ended up getting sick.

Alcohol was like a revelation. I was mourning my father and grandfather hard. The alcohol made it easier to think about other things. Alcohol helped me forget. Sometimes I would drink with older neighborhood kids, but mostly I carried my liquor-filled tennis-ball can into the woods alone.

By the age of twelve, I was also smoking pot. I once smoked a joint without knowing it was laced with PCP. I couldn't think straight. My eyes wouldn't focus. I stumbled home and mumbled something to my mom through the bedroom door before hiding in my room. After my father's death, she had taken to locking herself away in her bedroom all evening. This made it easier to sneak around. PCP was a scary experience. My brain felt utterly broken. I got in bed and pulled the covers over me and recited my own name and phone number for hours just to be sure that I still could.

My mom quickly caught on to what was happening. She could tell when I was sick from drinking. I came back from the woods one day and made a beeline to the bathroom. She followed me and stood in the doorway, taunting me while my head hung over the toilet.

"Is the room spinning?" she asked. "Do you feel good? Is this what you wanted?"

THE PROBLEM WITH MOM

I was used to my mom being critical, but not to her being quite this cruel. My grades had slipped a little while mourning my father and grandfather, but I was still doing okay in school. I had poured myself into sports. I played on every team that would have me. I was also making friends. Given everything I had endured, I was coping pretty well. I didn't see drinking and smoking pot as major problems. This was the 1980s. I was in high school. Everyone was drinking beer and smoking pot on the weekends.

I felt like nothing was ever good enough for my mom. She never offered praise, only criticism, and she became increasingly controlling. She had always been a little strict, but she really tightened the yoke when my dad got sick and again when he passed away.

In retrospect, it is clear that she felt like things were out of control, and she was just trying to control them. She was scared of losing her grip on everything. When things were chaotic or outside of her control, she would clamp down harder. She'd had no actual control over the course of my father's illness. But she was determined to at least maintain some semblance of control.

She wasn't well equipped to handle what was happening to our family. She'd started becoming irritable even before my father died. My dad was set up in the living room permanently by this point. We could all hear her crying alone for hours at a time. When she didn't work shifts at the hospital, she would stay holed up in her room. She became increasingly aloof. It felt like having an angry ghost in the house.

I realize this was all very hard on her. She was probably struggling financially. My mom worked, but my father had been the primary breadwinner. The loss of my father's income must have hit especially hard as his medical bills piled up. She was struggling to hold on to the house and raise two kids. That couldn't have been easy.

But things weren't easy for Kym and me either, and my mom was making everything much harder. She was critical when I needed understanding and love. She was controlling and stifling when I needed space or time with friends. She didn't want us seeing *anyone*. We weren't supposed to go to parties. She didn't want us having people over to the house. I wasn't allowed to date.

This was very hard on me. I had started dating a girl, my first love, in the eighth grade. My mom didn't want me seeing her. As an athlete, I was always getting invited to keg parties after sports games and pep rallies. I wasn't allowed to go to those either. I couldn't even have people over at the house when she was home. I could only have friends over when she was at work. If she came home early from the hospital to find people in the house, she would chase them out, yelling and screaming at the top of her lungs. Eventually, no one even *wanted* to come to my house. My friends thought my mom was crazy. And she was a reflection on me. Her weirdness made me feel like there was something wrong with *me*. I wanted to feel accepted, but I didn't feel accepted by my mom or by other kids.

I felt trapped and isolated in my own house. For years, having friends over was impossible because my dad had been in his hospital bed in the living room. Having people over felt like a violation of his privacy, even his dignity, when he was very sick. This was a reminder that my family was different, and not in a good way. My father was a good man, but he didn't always have the physical capacity to be a good father. He couldn't make it to games, couldn't come on the father-son Boy Scouts campout, and couldn't always tolerate people in the house when he was so sick. Now I couldn't have people over because my mom would freak out at them.

All of this contributed to me feeling like a freak myself. I was objectively popular and well liked, but I didn't *feel* that way. My family was weird, maybe even cursed, and so was I. While I was always smiling on the outside, on the inside I suffered from a prevailing sense of inadequacy. I put on a smile, but it was compensation for how bad I felt about myself. I started to think my mom was right—maybe there was nothing good about me.

I started to resent my mom. Nothing I did was ever good enough. I resented her constant disapproval. From my perspective, I wasn't being that bad. My friends were always sneaking out and drinking and smoking pot. Sometimes, they got in trouble. Sometimes, they got grounded. But their parents seemed so much cooler about everything than my mom. She was always on high alert whenever I left the house—if she would let me leave at all. I just wanted to go to parties like everyone else. I wanted to play sports, date girls, and have friends. I wanted to be normal. But she wouldn't let me do any of that. I felt oppressed by her. I even started believing all of the things she said about me. When you get a constant stream of criticism, especially at that age, it is impossible not to internalize some of it.

My sister was also struggling under our mother. She was two years older and felt even more stifled by our mom. Her friends were partying more. I smoked my first joint with her and her friends. We had something of a love-hate relationship. I was already six foot three in the eighth grade and attracting the attention of her girlfriends, which she didn't care for. Sometimes, Kym took out her frustrations on me. She could be very mean at times.

We were actually on a similar path at the time. We both partied a little much for teenagers, but not in a way that was particularly abnormal. This was the early 1980s. Rehab wasn't really part of the vernacular. Nancy Reagan hadn't launched her "Just Say No" campaign yet. My sister and I partied, but no one seemed to think we had a problem except for our mother.

Our grandmother didn't approve of the way she was treating us; neither did our mom's uncle, who lived nearby. Unfortunately, my mom did not take their opinions to heart. She thought we were messing up and that we needed more discipline than she could give. And she was about to do something drastic about it.

Chapter 3

TOUGH LOVE

COMMITTED

December 6, 1983

L osing my dad was hard. Losing my grandfather shortly there-after made things worse. But nothing could prepare me for what I went through as a teenager. Things hadn't been easy, but they were about to get a whole lot harder in the eighth grade.

Someone from the office came to pull me out of class. My mom was waiting for me. She took me out to the car.

"We're going to go for a ride," she said. "I want you to see a therapist."

Therapists were nothing new to me. I saw a therapist after my dad and grandfather died, but it had been a while since I had been to see him. There was no good reason for my mom to be taking me back again all of a sudden. I was still grieving. The same nagging sense of unworthiness and guilt that had plagued me for years hadn't gone away. I was very sad and insecure. But in my view, nothing had really changed.

Unfortunately, as I was about to find out, that wasn't *her* view.

We didn't talk in the car. My mom wouldn't say anything else. I sat quietly. I watched cars go by as she drove me thirty minutes across town. She parked in front of a big brick building that had clearly once been a grocery store. There wasn't any signage on the outside. The blinds were drawn down over all the windows so that you couldn't see inside.

"This is it?" I asked.

"Come on," my mom said, unbuckling her seat belt.

She led me inside and spoke to someone at the front desk. We sat in a waiting area until two teenage boys came to meet with us. My mom stayed up front while they took me to an office in the back. The room looked nothing like the inside of my old therapist's office. The walls were painted plain white. The room was basically empty except for a table and a few chairs. I was starting to get really creeped out.

The two boys did not go to get a therapist. Instead, they started questioning me about my drug use. They asked how much I was drinking, whether I smoked pot, what hard drugs I was doing. Why was I drinking every single day? How often did I drink in the morning? What was I getting high on? Cocaine? Pills? Heroin? What else? "Tell us everything you're using. Why do you take drugs?"

Their questions were so off base, so preposterously leading, that I didn't know how to answer. I was in high school. I smoked pot sometimes. I drank occasional beers. I played football and went to keg parties with the other guys on the team. None of this seemed that out of the ordinary. I drank, but no more than my friends, no more than my sister.

I didn't know who these two guys were or why they were

questioning me. They were too young to be therapists, maybe only a few years older than me. My neck had broken out in a sweat. I found it hard to focus on their questions. I wanted to know where my mom had gone. I was just thirteen years old. I was alone and scared. Why was I here?

What I didn't know at the time was that my mom had gotten involved with the tough love parenting movement that arose in the early 1980s. The movement advocated a no-nonsense, zero-tolerance approach to parenting teenagers with substance abuse issues or behavioral problems. The movement spawned a number of drug treatment centers that employed questionable behavior modification methods. In the 1970s, the federal government investigated some of these programs and found that many were engaging in outright abuse. Investigators caught many of them using brainwashing and torture tactics on kids in their so-called rehabilitation programs.

Many of these centers closed down due to investigations and bad press. People got arrested and went to jail. But new tough love rehabilitation centers kept popping up to take their places. Some centers rebranded and tapped into the fears created by the "Just Say No" and "tough on crime" rhetoric of the Reagan administration. One of the most notorious teen rehabilitation centers in the 1980s was Straight, Incorporated, which Nancy Reagan called her favorite antidrug program. They had branches in a few cities, including Atlanta, where my mother had taken me. Straight, Incorporated employed many of the same abusive practices as its predecessors and would eventually get shut down as well—but not in time to save me.

The two boys questioned me for what felt like hours. At some point, I realized they had positioned themselves between the door and me. They were holding me there against my will. My heart sank at the realization. I thought about bolting for the door, but they had several years on me and were much bigger. The room felt like an interrogation room. It *was* an interrogation room. The walls seemed to close in around me.

"I want to go home," I said.

"Well, you're not going home," they said. "You're staying here."

I could feel and hear the blood pumping in my ears. I didn't want to be there. I didn't even know where *there* was. While these kinds of rehabilitation centers were popping up all around the country, they operated under the radar. Rehab hadn't entered the popular lexicon yet. There was the Betty Ford Center, of course, and similar institutions for rich people, but the rehab industry was small. Going to rehab wasn't something the average person, much less the average *kid*, did in 1983. I didn't understand that places like this could hold you against your will.

> *Going to rehab wasn't something the average person, much less the average* kid, *did in 1983.*

At some point during the interrogation, my mom came into the room. This gave me hope that they would finally let me leave. Those hopes were quickly dashed. I had been kidnapped. And while I didn't know it yet, I would soon be abused and tortured.

My mom said that I was going to be staying there for a while. "This is going to be good for you. You need to embrace this."

She said goodbye in a way that made it clear she was not coming back. She left the room. I slumped down in my chair and continued answering questions. When the boys were done interrogating me, they took me to a large orientation room. It was filled with other teenagers. Many of them were in the same situation. Their eyes were glazed over and their expressions blank. They had been broadsided just as badly as I had.

Some didn't look shocked at all, just upset. I later learned that many of them had been through the program before, only to be brought back. Some of them had been through the program two or three times. Many of them had been there for months, some of them years.

This horrible reality was dawning on me. They were holding me prisoner, maybe for a very long time. There was no telling how long they planned to keep me there. Straight, Incorporated wasn't even a legitimate rehab. It operated more like an asylum. My mom had committed me here, and there was nothing I could do—no way to leave, no way to air grievances or argue my case. I was trapped.

The realization was dizzying. I teetered between anger and fear. I couldn't believe that my mom had just left me in that place.

INSIDE STRAIGHT, INCORPORATED
1983–1985

The staff was mostly teenagers who had been through the program themselves and then joined the staff. The counselors weren't licensed. They had no outside training. Most of them weren't even real employees. They were just teenagers—mostly troubled teenagers.

There were few adults on staff. There were a clinical director and a few other people managing the organization. They had private security. Abuse was rampant. The counselors had enormous power over every aspect of our daily lives. They lorded their power over us like the unchecked bullies they were. Imagine prisoners running the prison. That was basically the culture and structure of Straight, Incorporated.

Fifteen minutes after intake, they told us to take our seats while they explained the program and the rules. We weren't going home until we straightened out. We would be put through a seven-phase program that would transform us from alcoholics and drug addicts into functioning, respectable members of society. I was slouching down in my chair when a counselor punched me in the back.

"Sit up and have some self-respect," he snarled.

I spun around and stared him in the face. "Fuck off."

His eyes lit up with fire. There was a cruel grin on his face. It was clear that he was going to take joy in the provocation. Several of the counselors circled around and tackled me to the floor. They held me down while someone put his shoe on the back of my head and ground my face into the floor.

"You're going to learn how to behave around here," he said. "You're going to learn how to act right."

Fighting back was impossible with the weight of three or four boys on my back. I stopped struggling. However, I remained defiant the first few weeks. Being there drove me crazy. Being disrespected and bullied made me angry. Eventually, I would snap and act out. The counselors would lunge at the opportunity to pull me out of the group, take me into a back room, and start punching me in the face.

Straight demanded compliance. They expected us to admit to whatever we were accused of. I was taken into the bathroom by four boys once for acting out. They shoved me into a stall and pinned me against the wall.

"You are going to admit to being an addict and alcoholic, or you are going to be fed," one said.

They forced my head down into the toilet and held it underwater. "Admit it!" they shouted. "You are a loser drug addict! Admit it!"

"Yes!" I screamed out between gasps of toilet water and air. "I am an addict! I am an addict!" I would have said anything to keep them from drowning me in the toilet. I just wanted out. I was terrified, broken, alone, and desperate to feel safe and loved.

It became clear that compliance was the only way out—not just out of the bathroom stall but out of this nightmarish place. The first counselor to punch me had been right about one thing: I did learn how to *act*. There was nothing to do but swallow my pride and accept the helplessness of my situation. I stopped fighting back. I stopped acting out.

From then on, I did what I was told. I said whatever they wanted to hear. I knew what they wanted. In order to get out alive, I was going to have to work the program their way. I didn't argue with the counselors. I tried to stay off their radar. I didn't fight back or speak out. When bad things happened to other people, I tried not to think about what was happening. The whole thing was incredibly surreal.

The next few months were scary. Kids were getting beaten up all the time. What they did to us was awful. I heard kids crying out from beatings. They practically tortured us. The counselors weren't the only ones doing this kind of stuff. There were kids who would literally hold you upside down and dunk your head into the toilet so that you couldn't breathe anything but nasty water. We were encouraged to police each other. It was like *Lord of the Flies* from day one. You couldn't trust anybody—not the counselors, not the other kids in the program with you. They could snitch you out for anything.

I worked the program exactly how they wanted. I didn't want to be one of those kids locked away there for years. We attended group lessons several times a day. We would circle around and share stories about our addiction. They wanted us to raise our hands to be called on. We were supposed to admit to being addicts and alcoholics. I didn't think of myself as either at the time, but failing to participate in forced confession meant getting beaten down. I didn't want to find myself back in a bathroom stall with my head inside a toilet, so my hand was always one of the first up. When they called on me, I stood up and exaggerated my substance abuse. I told stories like the other kids were telling. I have no way of knowing who was just going through the motions like me.

I was traumatized by the experience. My mom had plucked me out of school one day, plucked me out of *life*, and left me in this terrifying place. We weren't even allowed to go to school. I spent all day at the rehabilitation center and nights with a host family. The center didn't have enough space for dorms, so they placed us with host families whose children were further along in the program. This allowed them to keep us isolated from friends and family at night. We went straight from the rehabilitation center to the host house at the end of the day. In the mornings, we were sent right back to the center.

We couldn't see or contact anyone outside of the program. During the first phases of the program, we weren't allowed to use the phone to call home. I hadn't talked to my mom since she walked out of the back office and left me there. Contacting anyone else for any reason was totally out of the question. My friends didn't even know what happened to me. One day I was in school; the next I just disappeared.

Even my girlfriend had no idea where I had gone. I was sure she was freaking out. I knew that my mother wouldn't tell her where I was. She thought my girlfriend was a bad influence on me. My mom thought everyone was a bad influence on me. I wished that I could just call my girlfriend and let her know that I was alive, but I had no way of doing so.

The only person from my life whom I could see was my sister. My mother checked Kym into the program a few weeks after me. But while I could *see* her, we weren't allowed to actually communicate.

The only time we saw each other was during group. Group therapy was held in one large room. They would break us into small groups and send us to different corners of the room. I was never put in the same group as Kym. During therapy, I could see Kym across the room. We would steal awkward glances at each other throughout the day but were never given the opportunity to talk. It was bizarre being able to see her daily but never talk. Several times every day, week after week, we would file into the same room for group, sometimes walking right past each other without ever exchanging a word. At the end of the day, she would be taken to her host family, and I would be taken to mine.

After a few weeks, I entered the second phase of the rehabilitation program and was finally allowed to phone home. Phone time was limited, and we weren't allowed to call anyone other than a parent or legal guardian. My only contact with the outside world was with my mother, who had put me into that hellhole. There was no one else. My father was dead. Kym and I were trapped in the center. It was just my mother on the other end of the line.

I honestly didn't even want to talk to her. I was seething with anger and felt totally violated. She had put me in there and she alone had the power to extricate me from the place. I was a minor. She was my guardian. Unless I wanted to wait until I was eighteen to get out of there, any path to freedom went through her. So I held my tongue. I forced a cheery disposition through clenched teeth and said what she wanted to hear. I treated her the same way I treated counselors. I said only what she wanted to hear. I said good things about the program and the center. I claimed to be making progress. Part of me doubted she would even believe me. Another part wondered if she even cared.

I used my time on the phone to fish for information. I was trying to understand why she had put me there. I asked about my grandmother and my friends. I wanted to know what she'd told my girlfriend. My mom was not forthcoming. I couldn't press too hard without seeming disobedient. I had to pretend not to care about my own real life. The risk of upsetting her was too high. I didn't want to be locked away in there forever.

As imperfect and hard as it had been, I missed my old life. I wanted to be back at high school. I wanted to see my friends and girlfriend. I wanted back on the football team. I wanted to go to games and pep rallies. I didn't want to miss out on prom or graduation. It felt like someone had stolen my life and that there was no way to get it back.

Pushed to my breaking point, I tried to escape. My host family was driving me back to Straight. Two of the counselors were riding along as security. When the car slowed at a light, I threw open the door and flung myself out of the car. I made a break for the woods, but the counselors caught up with me. They pummeled me on the side of the road and then dragged me back to the car. They sat on either side of me this time and held me down as we rode.

There was no escape. They had disappeared me.

There was no escape. They had disappeared me.

My father and grandfather were dead. They were both gone from my life. And now *I* was gone from my life. I was existing outside of time and place. It was like purgatory and hell wrapped up into one. At times, it felt like my life was a giant chaotic mess with me at the epicenter. At other times, it felt like my old life was receding away from me.

My old life got harder to remember. I could barely even remember a time that felt normal and good. My father as a healthy man was only a vague memory. Sometimes it was hard to remember his face from those days. I tried hard to hold on to those images of him in my mind, and of my grandfather too—the warmth and the happiness and the smiles. But it was hard, especially in that dark place.

Chapter 4

SIXTEEN AND HOMELESS

BACK HOME

1985

Keeping my head down, I worked my way through the residential phases of the program over the course of thirteen months. Most people stayed longer or ran away before finishing. I had convinced them that they had successfully brainwashed me. Despite my seething anger, I was able to keep cool. They moved me from phase to phase, believing that I bought into the program.

In the seventh and final phase, I graduated and was finally free. My feelings about going back home were mixed. I wanted out of Straight more than anything, but I wasn't keen on going back to my mom's house. Kym wouldn't be there. She didn't complete the program. She had managed to escape successfully and never came back. Going back home was out of the question. Kym moved in with her boyfriend and got a job.

That wasn't an option for me. I was only fourteen. I couldn't get a job or an apartment on my own. I had no choice but to go back home. I also wanted to finish high school. School was important to me. Normal people graduated from high school, and I wanted that.

Being back in the house was bizarre. I no longer trusted my mother. I felt betrayed and abandoned by her. I was also well aware that she had the power to send me back. I treated her like I'd treated the counselors at Straight. I did my best to stay out of her way. I avoided conflict as much as possible, though this was difficult. She would often come home from work angry about this or that. I tried to do what she wanted. I said what she wanted to hear. I would lie to make her happy.

Home life was bad. So was everything else. I had missed an entire year of school and had to start the eighth grade over again. My friends were all a year ahead of me now. They were in different classes and doing different things. It felt like everyone had moved on.

People at school treated me weird, even my old friends. *Especially* my old friends. No one had known where I was for the longest time. Suddenly, I was back, and it was like a ghost had returned.

My close friends had eventually figured out what had happened to me. They'd started tracking my mom's movements. They would follow her around town. They had figured out I was in Straight when she came to visit one day. Though mostly flying under the radar, Straight already had a bad reputation at the time. My friends tried to break me out one day, but counselors and security stopped them at the front and threw them out before calling the cops.

After that, my friends gave up. People did show concern. They asked where I had been. My friends gave me hugs and said they were happy to see me. But things were different now. They were freaked out by the whole ordeal. No one really went to rehab back in those days, certainly not young teenagers from middle-class families. They thought my mom was kind of "out there," but after my stint in rehab, some of them probably *did* believe that I had a serious drug problem too.

They were also afraid of my mom. My mom had always been antisocial and somewhat put off by my friends. Her behavior had put a bad taste in people's mouths. They stopped wanting to come over. No one could wrap their heads around her locking me up for a year in an institution. No one wanted to be around our family. We were weird and dysfunctional.

So I came back to school as a social pariah. I couldn't really blame them. My sister and I were fuckups who'd had to be sent away. It made total sense that people wouldn't want to be around me.

My girlfriend took my disappearance the hardest of all. We were only thirteen, but we did love each other. We were as serious as two thirteen-year-old kids can be. And then one day I just disappeared. I didn't call. I didn't write. She had no idea why. My mom called her mom and told her to keep her daughter away from me. She told her that her daughter was a bad influence on me, and that she didn't want her coming around the house.

My mom refused to tell her where I was or what had happened. She just said to stay away. This was so traumatizing to my girlfriend that her mom moved them to a different part of Atlanta and enrolled her in a different school district. We reconnected later in life, but it was a long time before we ever talked again. I wasn't unaware of the deep trauma this episode had caused her. It still pains me to this day.

I turned my back on my friends. Straight, Incorporated wanted us to cut off old friends when we went back home. The counselors emphasized how important it was to stay away from old friends who were a bad influence, which according to them was basically everyone. I didn't really want to do so, but I was also terrified of being sent back to rehab. There were lots of kids in the program doing their second or third tour of duty. The story was always the same. They would get out and start hanging out with the same people. They would go back to drinking and using until their parents put them right back in rehab.

While not really buying in to their indoctrination, I really didn't want to get sent back. I still felt alone and isolated. That nagging feeling of just wanting to belong and be loved and accepted was ever present. I wanted to stay free and be around people I loved. But this also meant avoiding anyone who smoked pot or drank alcohol, which in high school in 1984 was pretty much everyone. All the sports teams threw keg parties after games and pep rallies. I really couldn't participate in anything socially for fear my mom would find out that there had been drugs or alcohol at the party. So I stayed away.

> *Everyone was convinced that I had been brainwashed.... They thought I had joined a cult or something.*

This contributed to my alienation. Everyone was convinced that I had been brainwashed. I brought a copy of the Bible to school one day, and people kept side-eying me in class. They thought I had joined a cult or something. The Twelve Steps just weren't a part of the popular consciousness at the time. Being sober at fourteen was weird.

All this left me feeling very alone. After having just lost the two positive male role models in my life, I was shipped off to an environment so abusive that it would be shut down by federal investigators a few short years later. The abuse was so bad that there are still active support groups for Straight, Incorporated survivors all across the country. The way they treated us was unequivocally child abuse. I struggle to remember details now because it was so traumatizing. My brain just hit the delete button on most of my memories. I was struggling to work through what had just happened to me. And then I was back at home, living with the person who had sent me there. I couldn't trust my mother, not after what she had done. My sister had run away from home. I had no friends. I'd lost my girlfriend.

At times, I would lie in bed, feeling like I couldn't even breathe. The whole world felt alien and my body like a husk. I felt disconnected from everything. In school, I rarely talked despite formerly being an outgoing person. At home, I holed up in my room to avoid my mom. I was isolated and alone with my thoughts. I felt crazy. The years kept replaying in my head, each one worse than the one before. I was only fourteen years old and dying inside.

FROM COUCH TO COUCH

1985–1986

While Straight, Incorporated did basically everything wrong, they did succeed in getting me to give up drinking and smoking pot. Straight had scared me straight. I was so afraid of being sent back that I wouldn't touch alcohol or drugs. I tried to stay away from people who drank. For the first six months back at the house, I was completely sober.

Staying sober got harder over time, though. I was carrying a lot of trauma around with me. Drinking and smoking pot were how I dealt with that trauma. I had to find new ways to cope.

Even harder was giving up drinking as a social activity. I was in high school. Some people go to school and don't drink alcohol or take drugs, but that was the only way I knew how to relate with people. I was heavily involved in sports, and high school athletes are known for heavy drinking. The peer pressure was intense. It felt impossible to have a social life without at least social drinking.

I tried to stay away from the temptation, but that was isolating. When I did go to drinking events sober, other kids thought it was weird. This made it even harder to be around people. I felt like a freak for having been sent to rehab. Now I felt like a freak for being sober.

So I went back to drinking. I was at a party one night, and everyone else was drinking. I felt out of place and alone. My personal heroes were both dead. I was still reeling from physical and mental abuse at rehab. My mom was an authoritarian who never showed me any love. I didn't have any real friends anymore. I felt so out of place at the party. I just wanted to feel normal again. So I started drinking too.

Things escalated from there. It wasn't just the drinking. It was my mom. She found out I had been drinking at a party and threw me out of the house. There wasn't any talk about going back to rehab, which had been my greatest fear. She just wanted me out the door. I grabbed a few things and stormed out of the house. I stayed the night at a friend's house.

The next few years were extremely chaotic. I was homeless at sixteen. I spent months at a time bouncing around on couches and raiding the fridge when my friends' parents were out of the house. I stole food from grocery stores and gas stations. Sometimes I went to my grandmother's house for a meal, but she was in her seventies and couldn't offer me a place to stay. She wasn't equipped to take in a teenage boy.

Some of my friends were sympathetic. They thought my mom was crazy and wanted to help. We were all kids, though. It wasn't like they could take me in. They would let me stay for a few nights here and there. I rotated houses, crashing somewhere new almost every night, for as long as I could.

Their parents caught on quickly. Some of them took pity on me, but they also didn't want to get mixed up with the law. It's no small thing to take in a minor. My mom could have told the police that I was a runaway. So while I had friends willing to let me sleep over, their parents didn't want me staying for longer than a night or two. I would sleep on the couch or in a sleeping bag. After a couple of days, they would hint that it was time to move on.

One friend let me sleep in his basement. I would either get up early to sneak away before his parents got up or hide until they left for work. Eventually they caught me, and that lifeline was gone.

Eventually, you run out of places to crash. There were many nights that I had nowhere to go. When that happened, I would have no choice but to sleep outside. I often slept in the woods where I used to go to sneak drinks.

Throughout all of this, I was still trying to keep up with school. I really didn't want to drop out. School had the practical benefit of giving me a safe place to be during the day. Being out on the street opened me up to being harassed or picked up by the police. Going to school had psychological benefits as well. Being homeless made me feel weird and isolated. It made me feel like there was something wrong with me, that I was less than everyone else and completely unworthy of love. Going to school gave me some small sense of normalcy when everything else was so chaotic and abnormal. Sitting at my

My one burning desire was just to be normal.

school desk, I could blend in with all the other kids leading normal lives. In class or at practice, I could at least pretend to be like everyone else. My one burning desire was just to be normal.

So I did my best to keep up with classes despite being homeless. I stayed on my sports teams. Sports gave me a sense of competency and control that was completely absent in the rest of my life. On the court, I had a sense of purpose and a tribe. I felt accepted when passing a ball to a teammate. This was not something I wanted to give up, no matter how hard things got. It didn't matter if I had spent the night hunkered down alone in the woods, sleeping on the ground, with no way to take a shower. I was still going to make basketball practice. I wasn't going to miss the soccer match.

Try as I might, though, I did miss classes. My grades did suffer. Studying and doing homework are hard when you don't have a reliable roof over your head. There was nothing to do, though, but push through. I did everything I could to pass classes. I wanted to make it to graduation. Living on the street was a bizarre life. It felt like someone else's life, not mine. I was from a middle-class suburban background.

Finding a place to stay every night got harder as time went on. My friends' parents, even some of my friends, started to lose patience. You can only ask so much of people. I started spending more and more nights outside, which got to be unbearable. I was starting to *look* more and more like a homeless person.

When things got bad enough, I would go back to my mom's house and beg her to let me stay. Her house was always a place of last resort. I had not forgiven her for sending me to Straight or throwing me out of the house. I blamed her for much of what was happening to me. I really hadn't been that bad of a kid. Why *not* drink when you're sleeping outside under a tree? My life was terrible and hard for a sixteen-year-old kid. And she was playing an active role in making things hard for me when she should have been showing love and a little care. While my view was possibly distorted by inner pain and resentment, this is how it seemed to me at the time.

I really didn't want to go back home. For all intents and purposes, home no longer existed. My father was dead. My sister had run away. I had been thrown out. There was just my mom's house, which was not a good place and didn't have any of the qualities of home. The house was a place of fear and control, not warmth and love. I really didn't want to go back.

But sleeping outside in the heat and humidity and bugs wasn't great either. I eventually hit the end of my rope and went back to my mom's house. I begged her to let me stay in my old room. She decided to give it a try. We started fighting almost immediately. She would come home from work mad about something. She would start yelling. Then I would start yelling. We were always shouting at each other. Eventually, she threw me out of the house again.

These fights could be bad, explosive, but they were also routine. I would eventually come back and apologize. She would call a truce. Nothing really bad came of these fights until one night she picked up the phone and dialed 911 in the middle of an argument. She told the dispatcher that I was terrorizing her. Police showed up at the house, and my mom had me arrested. The officers slapped a pair of handcuffs around my wrists and loaded me into the back of a squad car. I spent the night locked up in juvenile detention.

Straight, Incorporated had effectively been a prison, but it at least looked more like a school or government building. Juvenile detention looked like an actual prison. They put me in a small cell. The floor was concrete. The walls were concrete. The room wasn't much wider than the length of my body. There was a bed to sleep on and not much else. Being in the cell was like being inside a tomb.

I felt helpless and trapped. I stayed up all night, wondering how I had gotten there. How had I gone from being supposedly "gifted" in the first grade to being homeless and locked up in a cell at sixteen? I kept turning the question over in my head. How had I gotten there? What had gone wrong? It honestly didn't make any sense. I was just a normal suburban kid. I wasn't supposed to be in jail.

Except I *was* in jail. This was just more proof that there was something wrong with me. My life wasn't normal. I wasn't normal. Good kids don't go to jail, so I must be bad—it was flawed logic, an incomplete truth, but convincing in its simplicity.

I imagined what my father or grandfather would think of me locked up in a cell. Would they be disappointed? Who would they be angry with, my mom or me? I didn't really know. I blamed my mom. But it was impossible not to internalize blame for what was happening to me. My mom wasn't wrong. I was drinking. I was smoking pot. I didn't think I deserved this treatment, but maybe I was wrong. Why else did things keep going wrong? I was the main constant in my own life, of course, so I blamed myself as often as I blamed her.

I thought back to my elementary school teacher who had commented on the death of my father and grandfather. *God, Steve, who is going to die next?* It was a fair question—what was coming next? If the past was any indication of the future, it wasn't going to be good.

I spent only one night in detention. The police released me the next day. After having been arrested, I wasn't going back to my mom's house. I went back to couch hopping instead. I went back to struggling to hold things together. I went back to school. I went back to sleeping in the woods. I went from one couch to the next. I felt so very old and tired.

Somehow, despite all of this going on, I was able to pass all my classes and stick with my teams. I played both basketball and soccer that year and did well in both. It was hard but totally worth the effort—and one of the few good things in my life.

LIFE ON THE STREETS

Summer 1986

Things got even more difficult when school let out for the summer. I no longer had a place to be during the day. My evenings weren't taken up by games and practices. There weren't any rallies or after-parties. Suddenly, I had nowhere to be. It was one thing to stay with friends in the evenings and on weekends, but I couldn't just hang around all day, every day, without upsetting their parents. I now had to spend more of my days out on the streets, walking around the suburbs, and it was getting hot. Some days were up over a hundred degrees, and the air would get so thick with humidity you could almost bite down on it.

The bigger issue was being visibly homeless in the suburbs, especially as a minor. I was likely to attract the attention of cops. There aren't a lot of homeless kids sleeping outside in upper middle-class suburbs. I decided that it would be easier to keep a low profile in the city. Without school in session, there was nothing tying me to the suburbs anyway. So I got a ride into the city with some friends.

My hunch was correct. In the suburbs, I drew stares. In Atlanta, respectable society didn't bother or even notice me. There were homeless people everywhere, and lots of them looked a lot rougher around the edges than me. During the day, no one could even tell I was homeless as long as I didn't loiter in the same place too long. I was just another kid out in the city, at least during the day, which honestly felt good. It helped me maintain the illusion of normality that was so important to me.

Nights were a different story. Staying in the city made it easier to keep a low profile during the day, but it also made things more dangerous after dark. There was a lot more to worry about than just the police. They wouldn't hassle me in the city, but there were other people on the street who could pose a threat. Lots of other people struggling with addiction and mental health issues end up on the streets. They aren't all safe to be around. I was just a scared kid, and I very much looked the part. I would have made an easy victim.

While blending into crowds during the day helped me feel more normal, being forced to sleep in squats and encampments for the homeless had the opposite effect. There is really no denying that your life has taken a wrong turn when you find yourself sleeping in alleys and behind bushes.

I started sleeping in an abandoned house in midtown Atlanta. The place smelled foul. The stench of piss and old sweat hung in the air. The house was a squat. There were homeless people—*other* homeless people, I should say—revolving in and out of the house. There were winos and drug addicts and teenage runaways all under one roof. I never felt safe at night, and sleeping was hard, but it was better than being alone and exposed outside on the street.

These were some of my darkest days. I was living in places that I never could have imagined. I was living a life that didn't seem like mine. I was doing things that I never thought I would do.

A new low came when I ran into someone I knew from Straight, Incorporated while walking the streets. We stopped and started talking. He was a meth addict, and it was clear that he was tweaking. He kept working his jaw while we talked. I told him my parent had thrown me out of the house. He told me the same. We laughed. He had scraped together enough money for a cheap hotel room downtown and offered to let me crash there.

The place was a total dump, maybe the cheapest room in all of Atlanta, but it was far better than the squat house. The hotel room was at least private. There was a lock on the door and someone down at the front desk.

I stayed at the hotel for three days. He was shooting up crystal meth and asked me if I wanted to try it. I had never done hard drugs before. In school, we had talked about injection drug use. "Just Say No" was pretty corny, but never did I think I would shoot up drugs. I thought of drugs like that as wholly different from pot or alcohol. None of my high school friends did hard drugs. I didn't know anyone who had until going to Straight. Listening to kids talk about shooting heroin or crystal seemed so crazy and outside my world. I remember thinking that *they* were the real addicts, not me, and that there was no way I would touch that stuff.

I barely even had to think about it before saying sure. That should have been an alarm, loud and clear, that I was already an addict. I always normalized pot and alcohol. My relationship with them was always problematic. I would drink and smoke pot to mask my pain, not just to have fun, but since everyone was doing the same things, it was easy to normalize it. That day should have absolved me of any confusion over whether I had a substance abuse problem. There is nothing normal about loading a syringe with drugs and shooting them into your arm. And I did it the first time someone put a needle and some meth in front of me. This should have disabused me of any notion that I wasn't already an addict on the make.

I didn't care, though. I was dirty and tired. My life was a wreck. I was happy to do anything that would make me forget about my problems. So I picked up the needle. I found a vein like he showed me and depressed the plunger. A euphoria like nothing I had ever experienced hit me within seconds. I understood immediately why people shoot up.

The euphoria of the drug wasn't enough to keep me from feeling lost in every conceivable way, though. I was the most lost I had ever been. I had never thought of myself as someone who would even touch a needle. Crossing that line was incontrovertible proof that there was nothing I wouldn't do to get high. My life had come to this, and there was no denying it. I was overcome with a deep sense of shame.

Crossing that line was incontrovertible proof that there was nothing I wouldn't do to get high.

I was tweaking so hard that I didn't sleep for two nights. Afterward, I crashed hard. I must have slept twenty-four hours straight. When I came to, we had to leave. He only had the room for a few days. That was probably a blessing in disguise. Being back on the streets wasn't great, but holing up in a meth den would have been worse. I have no doubt that I would have kept using meth if it had been sitting around. I was willing to take anything that would turn off my mind and make me forget the state of my life.

THE PAUL ANDERSON
YOUTH HOME

1987

I went back to bouncing around from place to place. Eventually, I ended up back in the suburbs and back at my mom's house. I had been dealing with homelessness and unstable housing for about six months at that point. I was exhausted. My mental state was a wreck. I just needed off the street, even if just for a little while. Even if it meant going back home.

The front door was locked. I went around back and found her in the yard. She was angry. "Where have you been?"

The tone of her voice pissed me off. "I was out shooting up," I snapped. "You want to see the track marks?" I was trying to make her feel guilty.

We started fighting. I stormed away and into the house. I went to my old bedroom and locked the door behind me. She called the police again. When they showed up at the house, she made up some story about me destroying her property. I hadn't broken anything, but it didn't matter. She was willing to say whatever to get me arrested again. The police took what she said at face value. They took me away and locked me up in juvenile detention again.

By the time they released me to go back home, my mom had come up with a new plan for me. She wanted me to go away to the Paul Anderson Youth House in Vidalia, Georgia. This was a Christ-centered shelter for struggling boys founded by Paul Anderson, an Olympic gold medalist in weightlifting who had made the *Guinness Book of World Records*. The home was one of his passion projects.

I felt so unwanted. My mom was always tossing me out of the house. First, she'd sent me away to Straight, Incorporated. Twice now she had called the police to haul me off. And now she wanted to pack me off to live downstate.

My rage was palpable. Why had I been so easy to throw away? Maybe she couldn't deal with us after my father's death? Maybe she had never wanted to adopt kids in the first

> *My rage was palpable. Why had I been so easy to throw away?*

place? I didn't know. I just felt so discarded. Things changed after my father died. I understand that this was traumatic for her also, but the fact that she had been trying to pawn me off on someone else ever since made me wonder if adoption had been my dad's idea alone.

I agreed to go to the youth shelter. My mom didn't want me

in the house. I didn't want to be in her house. It just made sense to go away. My life had become an unmanageable downward spiral. I didn't want to keep cycling through couches and squats and jails. I was tired. I had turned sixteen, and my life felt completely derailed. Getting out of Atlanta and into stable housing for a little while didn't sound bad.

After my experience with Straight, Incorporated, I was scared of entering another youth rehabilitation center. Thankfully, the Paul Anderson Youth Home was totally different. They functioned more like a Christian boarding school for troubled youth. We stayed in dorms, helped with chores, and took classes. The rehabilitation center opened its own accredited school that focused on college prep and getting kids into training programs. Many of the graduates ended up going into the military. It was focused on reforming behavior and ushering problem children to the next phase of their life.

Unlike Straight, the staff and teachers really wanted to help. They were good people. They were kind and compassionate. They didn't abuse us. They really worked to help troubled young people get their lives back together.

A lot of the kids were there because they had alcohol and drug problems. The program placed a heavy focus on behavior modification. They didn't treat me like an addict so much as a misbehaved kid. Today, the recovery community is focused on healing and learning how to live without drugs and alcohol. Most alcohol and drug rehabilitation programs help addicts get to the root of the problems that drive them to substance abuse. That was not how Paul Anderson Youth Home approached drug use, at least at the time. They treated drinking and drugging the same as any other problematic behaviors that needed correcting. They didn't care why I drank or did drugs—they just wanted me to stop.

The program was very Christ centered. We attended church every day. There were Bible classes in addition to our regular academic classes. They were trying to make us into better people by helping us become good Christians. None of this was alien to me. I had been raised in the church. I had participated in youth groups before, though I never stuck with it. I never bought into the "fire and brimstone" versions of Christianity and still don't, but I did have a personal relationship with God. I would speak to him often in those early years of my life when everything seemed to be going wrong all the time. I didn't understand why all these bad things kept happening to me. I actually felt unloved by God at the time. I didn't have the capacity to understand that bad things happen to good people, and so when bad things kept happening to me, I took it as a sign that I was a bad person and that God didn't love me.

My first six months at Paul Anderson were mostly good. I had gone so long without stable housing or caring adults in my life that living in a dorm was a relief. I had the structure of class schedules. We did chores and maintained the property, which gave me a little sense of purpose. For the first time in a while, I felt safe and secure.

I was in a better place, but I still felt isolated. I was in a tiny rural town in the middle of nowhere. The nearest cities were hours away. I missed my friends in Atlanta. And I didn't really know why I was there other than that it had been convenient. I didn't have a religion problem. I felt angry that my mom had coerced me into going there.

Eventually, I decided to leave. I didn't even make it through the whole year. There was another kid from Atlanta who wanted to run away too. We decided to travel together. I packed my things one night before bed, and we sneaked off in the dark. We hitchhiked all the way back to Atlanta in the dead of night. I was back in the city before they even knew we were gone.

Chapter 5

BACK IN THE CITY

BACK TO USING,
BACK TO REHAB

1988

I was seventeen years old and very angry about life when I came back to Atlanta. I had been a sad and depressed kid. I was becoming an angry teenager. The whole world just seemed like one big fuck you. The two most important men in my life had died. My mom had abandoned me. I had been physically and mentally abused. My sister and I had drifted apart. I still didn't understand why these things had happened, but I knew that I was angry about them.

My anger was the main reason I couldn't stay at Paul Anderson. It was a Christian youth home. I was feeling pretty angry with God. I felt isolated and unlovable, even by God. After so many bad years, I was losing hope that things would ever get better. I didn't really want to hear about how God would make my life better. My life was crap, and God hadn't helped me one bit.

A man without hope is a dangerous thing. Back in Atlanta, I turned to all my favorite vices. I no longer cared about anything. I was back to being homeless and couch hopping. I was caught in an endless cycle of despair, discomfort, and instability. Drugs and alcohol were the easiest way to numb myself to reality. I started drinking again, more heavily this time. I no longer stuck to pot. I was happy to take any drugs I could get my hands on. I got heavily into party drugs. I was dropping acid and ecstasy regularly. When I found cocaine, it was another revelation. Here was this simple white powder I could snort and be on top of the world.

Needless to say, I got myself into bad shape quickly. Talking to my mom during this period was difficult. I avoided her entirely. I didn't even go to the house. But I felt bad not letting her know that I was alive. After being back in Atlanta for six drug-fueled weeks, I gave her a call from a friend's house.

She wanted me to go back to the youth house in the country.

"I'm not going to a Christian school," I said. "I don't have a religion problem."

Maybe I didn't have a religion problem, but I did have a drug and alcohol problem. There was no longer any denying that. No one was fooled, not even me. I had real problems, and they were drug problems.

My mom was able to convince me to check into rehab. This was partly through coercion. I had been sent to the Paul Anderson facility under court order. I was still only seventeen and technically a runaway. My mom could have reported me to the police. I didn't want to get picked up by cops, especially with pocketsful of drugs, so I agreed to rehab.

I wanted to go. My life was a mess, and something had to change. I had experienced a hard six weeks. I was apparently incapable of staying sober on my own. My life was just one big cycle of chaos, and I wanted to put an end to it. That wasn't going to be possible while taking drugs and getting drunk all the time.

It felt like time was running out to make that change. There were going to be consequences for living this way. At seventeen, I was almost an adult. I wasn't going to be able to crash on couches for the rest of my life. I was going to need to get a job and get my shit together. Otherwise, I was going to end up like the older kids at Straight: a burnout in my twenties. I didn't want that for myself. I was terrified of it, actually. I agreed to give rehab another try.

I told myself that this wasn't forever. I just needed to get clean and get my life on track. Then I could go back to drinking and smoking pot like a normal person. The insane bargaining that takes place in addiction is

> *The insane bargaining that takes place in addiction is endless—anything to avoid the truth.*

endless—anything to avoid the truth. Giving up alcohol forever was a tough pill to swallow at seventeen. I just wanted to be normal. In my mind, normal people drank and smoked pot. They just did it like normal people. They didn't binge for days on end. They didn't drink all day. They certainly didn't stick a needle in a vein and shoot up crystal meth on a whim. But they did drink. Sometimes they smoked pot or dropped pills at the nightclub. Those things seemed like an important part of being a normal young adult.

Not everyone did drugs or drank, but they did in my world. In retrospect, I can see that this was the same old rationalizing that all addicts do. But at the time I really believed it was possible to drink in a normal way. I told myself that if I could just get clean for a while, it would prove that I didn't have a problem. This was the insane bargaining that comes with addiction—it's endless. You make a deal with yourself, you break it, then you make another. The back-and-forth allows you to deny the truth indefinitely. It's always anything to avoid the truth.

Despite my hesitance to give up alcohol and drugs forever, I did want things to cool down. I knew that what I was wasn't normal. My life was so chaotic. It wasn't just the drugs and alcohol. It wasn't just living on the streets. It wasn't just the loss and the mourning. It was everything. Though I wouldn't have used the word at the time, my life had become unmanageable. My hope was that rehab would give me a firm footing to make some real changes.

I agreed to give rehab a try as long as it wasn't a radical tough love program. My mom checked me into Addiction Recovery of Chattanooga (ARC), an inpatient rehab in Tennessee, for a six-week program. This was a standard Twelve Steps program focused on understanding why we drank and used drugs. It was nothing like Straight, Incorporated. The methodology was coherent and sane. The counselors were actual adults. They didn't abuse us. And unlike the Paul Anderson Youth House, they helped me work through some of my feelings. My time there was short, but it was good to be away from drugs and alcohol. Overall, I had a positive experience. I got sober. I did a little healing and worked through some of my problems. My perspective shifted. I had gone in just hoping for a break from my life. To my surprise, I came out not wanting to drink anymore. I wanted to actually stay sober.

THE MUSIC SCENE

1988

After six weeks, I finished the program. My mom and stepfather didn't want me coming back home afterward. My stepdad was not interested in my life at all. My mom didn't want to deal with me anymore. Sending me downstate had been a way to keep me out of her hair while putting me someplace safe. That's probably why she sent me to Straight as well. We could never get on the same page. I was sober now, but there was no reason to think our relationship would change. She didn't want to deal with my problems anymore.

The recovery program helped me get into a halfway house in Atlanta. I was there for six months. As part of my living arrangement, I was required to get a job. It was time to start thinking more about what I wanted out of life. I was almost an adult. I didn't finish high school, which meant employment options were limited. I ended up taking a lot of odd low-skill jobs. I was particularly interested in working in the music industry.

I was able to work my way into Atlanta's music scene by working security at rock concerts. One of my first jobs was at the Center Stage Theater in Atlanta. They hired me to do odd jobs. I worked the doors. I swept up. I helped some of the stagehands. My first gig was working stage security for the Ramones. It was a sold-out show. I had seen *Rock 'n' Roll High School* but didn't really know much about the band. I was more into metal and hard rock. My job was to stay up front and keep people away from the band and the monitors. When people climbed the stage to crowd-surf, I would push them back into the pit. The energy was palpable. I was hooked.

This was an exciting time to be in the music industry. There were new scenes popping up all over the country, including Atlanta.

Locally, the Atlanta scene was blowing up in the 1980s. The Black Crows and Collective Soul were both about to get signed. Over in Athens, the B-52s had gotten big, and REM was about to break. There was a lot of energy in a lot of scenes. Punk and hard core were getting popular. Heavy metal was no longer just underground. I grew my hair out long and started dressing like a metalhead.

Working shows was the most exciting thing I had ever done. I was there when Dead Kennedys and the Circle Jerks played Atlanta. I worked the Roxy the night Skid Row came to town. I was on stage setting things up when their lead singer, Sebastian Bach, came into the theater. Seeing him in the flesh was strange. At twenty-one years old, he had only a few years on me, but he was fronting a band that had just put out a multiplatinum debut record. The video for "Youth Gone Wild" was the number one video on MTV. And here he was, standing before me in the flesh. I'll never forget how he introduced himself. He walked up to me and spit on the ground at my feet. "Hey, I'm Sebastian," he said. "I just spit half a gram of cocaine at your feet." It was totally outlandish, and I thought it was so cool.

Working music venues gave me a new sense of purpose. I felt a part of something, if only a small part. I was excited to be around big, national acts. I liked seeing local bands break. I wanted to manage bands. Working venues allowed me to network while putting a little cash in my pocket. I wasn't making much, but having my own money for the first time felt good. It helped that I wasn't blowing any of it on alcohol and/or drugs.

In the evenings, I went to Narcotics Anonymous meetings. I started hanging out with a group of kids my age who were also trying to stay sober. Some of them were in the straight-edge scene, which was a reaction to all of the drugs and alcohol in the punk scene. Others were just kids who were trying to stay sober. None of them did drugs or drank alcohol, which helped me stay sober too. I had my own little tribe of long-haired metalheads who were sober. It made not drinking a lot easier, especially at shows. The music scene was soaked in booze and steeped in drugs. It was good to have people in the scene who weren't about that lifestyle. We would go to shows and Twelve Steps meetings together and then hang out afterward. I got an apartment with some of them when I got out of the halfway house.

My life began to stabilize. I was totally sober for a year and a half. Life felt more and more normal. I was still living in a halfway house, which could be embarrassing to tell people, but I was sober and doing interesting work. I had a roof over my head. My mother was no longer in my life. I began to realize just how responsible she was for our toxic relationship. My resentments ran deep, and it was impossible to forgive and forget. I stopped blaming myself for how things were between us. For the most part, I cut her out of my life.

Unfortunately, the sobriety didn't last. After eighteen months, I started drinking again. It was hard to stay sober while working in the music scene. And I was getting really into the scene. My gig at Center Stage had led me into managing bands. I wasn't good on an instrument at the time, so I worked to develop and manage bands. I knew a lot of musicians and had connections at the local venues. At one point, I was managing four or five bands at a time. We would play local shows wherever we could get gigs—the Masquerade, the Roxy, all the joints. I booked regional tours so that they could get exposure in other towns. Athens was a big music town, having broken as many bands as much larger Atlanta, and there were also smaller scenes in Savannah and Charleston.

I wasn't making much money. We were small fry. The dream was for one of them to get signed to a national label so that we could all quit our day jobs. In the meantime, I was working back-of-house restaurant jobs and doing odd gigs to pay the bills. My most consistent work was with restaurant chains. I worked the flattop grill at Steak 'n Shake. I was a line cook at a Fuddruckers. I did a stint in the kitchen at a Houston's Restaurant.

The music scene was fun, but it wasn't good for my sobriety. Staying clean and sober got harder and harder. I was in clubs and bars several nights a week. Sometimes I would go on tour with my friends, and people would be drinking in the van or on stage. It also didn't help that I was working in restaurants, where drinking every night was the norm. People would go out drinking after shifts, and it was hard to make friends unless you went out drinking with them.

On top of all that, several of the guys in my clique of sober musicians went back to drinking. They fell to the same pressures that I did. Some of the others drifted away. My sober tribe was falling apart. Without a recovery program or community, sobriety felt isolating. I wasn't even going to Twelve Steps meetings anymore. The busier I got with my bands, the less time I had for that and the further away I felt from rehab. I started to tell myself that I had never really had a *real* drinking problem anyway. I was seeing everyone around me having a good time, and I wanted that too.

I started drinking at shows. One night, I was in a club while one of my bands was totally blasted and having so much fun. I was over in a corner, feeling out of place. I said to hell with it and ordered a drink at the bar. This is what people do, I told myself, convinced that drinking normally was possible.

Of course, it wasn't possible. My drinking and using picked up almost right where things had left off. Within a few months, I wasn't just having a drink at shows. I was getting drunk at shows. I was back to smoking pot. I was back to dropping acid and ecstasy. Snorting cocaine became as casual as having drinks. There wasn't a drug I wouldn't take so long as it didn't involve shooting up.

My days and weeks started to blur into one another. I was doing hard drugs five or six days a week. It was "anything goes" every night. Sometimes I stayed up for days at a time, high on cocaine or crystal meth. Sometimes, I would go on marathon trips. I would be hallucinating for days at a time. Sometimes just the sleep deprivation was enough to have me seeing things that weren't there. My mind felt bent and fried, but I would push through and do it again the next weekend. Sometimes the next day.

This is when my addictions really started to get out of hand. There was no longer any plausible deniability about being an alcoholic and drug addict. I wouldn't

There was no longer any plausible deniability about being an alcoholic and drug addict.

have admitted so, usually not even to myself. I just pushed thoughts like that out of my mind and buried them under more drugs. I told myself this was what rockers did. It was just the lifestyle. I was living the rock 'n' roll lifestyle, and there was nothing wrong with that.

But it wasn't true. I wasn't even a rock star. I wasn't a big-shot producer or manager. I was just a twenty-year-old kid totally strung out on drugs. I just couldn't think about things that way, because it was too painful. My life was a mess. I was a mess. But I didn't want to deal with that. I just kept telling myself we'd get a record deal one day and that everything would be okay—better than okay. I just had to hang in there. And, in the meantime, party.

"GOD, STEVE, WHO'S NEXT?"

1989

This went on for about a year and a half, until I got a call from my sister. I don't even know how she got hold of me. I was out in Savannah, Georgia, for a gig. This was before cell phones or email. Somehow, she managed to get the number for one of the clubs we were playing, and they gave her the number for the house I was crashing at with the band.

"Kym?" I said, surprised to hear her on the other end of the line. We had not kept in touch. She was living in Charleston with her husband.

"Mimi is dead," she said. "You need to come home."

It was shocking to hear that my grandmother was dead. I hadn't seen her in a long time. She was one of the most important people from my childhood, but I hadn't wanted her to see me this way. When my mom threw me out of the house, I could go to her place for a hot meal and warm company. While she didn't approve of how my mom was handling Kym and me, there was nothing she could do to help. It wasn't like she could take me in. She was well into her seventies. She wasn't equipped to take in a teenage boy. And she didn't understand my problems. Trauma and addiction were alien concepts to her. Drugs weren't a part of her world. She would always ask me why I wouldn't just do the right thing and get along with my mother. "Why can't you just be good, Steve?" It was a hard question to answer, because I didn't think I was good. As much as I blamed my mother, I also blamed myself. I couldn't be good because in my mind, I wasn't good.

I felt torn on the inside. I didn't want to go home and see family. I didn't want to be seen by family either, not in the state that I was in.

They would know right away that I had been living hard. But I also wasn't going to miss my grandmother's funeral.

She gave me the date and the location. After the gig, I packed my things and headed back to Atlanta alone.

The funeral was surreal. I must have looked so out of place with my hair down to my shoulders. Even dressed up for the funeral, I very much looked the part of a rocker from the 1980s. It was uncomfortable being there, but I was glad I went. My grandmother had meant the world to me. I loved her and my grandfather, and now they were both gone. It really felt like I didn't have a family anymore, even as I sat at the funeral surrounded by family. Kym and I were so alienated. I couldn't even look at my mother. I was still so angry with her. We hadn't talked in years. I'd stopped calling when I moved into the halfway house in Atlanta. We didn't want anything to do with each other. She had remarried and wanted to move on with her new life. I was bitter and wounded and found it impossible to forgive her.

They sat me down at my mom's house a few days after the funeral to talk about the inheritance my grandmother had left me. It wasn't a lot of money, but it was something. The money wasn't going to be issued in a lump sum, which was probably a blessing, as I might have blown it all on drugs. The executor of her estate was going to dole out the money over time. He was there. So were Kym and my mom. I hated being in the same room with her.

Kym wanted me to come live with her while I got my life back together. She said she wanted us to be closer. She was living in Charleston with her husband. They had a house. She made her life sound perfect. I would later find out that this was a farce, but I didn't know any better. In my mind, she was a pillar of stability compared to me.

"Come to Charleston," she said. "Stay with us while you get back on your feet."

The executor of my grandmother's estate said that he was willing to give me enough money from the estate to pay for college. But I had to leave Atlanta. I had to cut my hair short and get a job. This wasn't really framed as a choice. He had some control over how the money would be doled out. If I wanted enough money for college, I was going to have to play by their rules.

I was torn. Leaving Atlanta meant walking away from my whole life. But truth be told, it wasn't a great life. I was drinking and drugging way too hard. I was having a lot of fun, but deep down inside I knew that this wasn't a sustainable life. I was getting older. There wasn't any future in staying up for days at a time, hallucinating out of my mind, and being hungover and strung out all the time.

Things were getting pretty bad, and Atlanta had left a foul taste in my mouth. The city was full of painful memories. Atlanta was drinking and drugs and homelessness. Atlanta was my mother. Atlanta was my dead father and grandfather. Atlanta was being yanked out of school and getting abused at Straight, Incorporated.

I could see that Atlanta was going to have me back out living on the streets again.

The only things I had going for me in Atlanta were my bands, and none of them were taking off. My obsession with the music industry was leading me back down the path of addiction. All of my friends, even the once-sober friends I was living with, were on drugs and partying all the time. In sober moments, I could see that Atlanta was going to have me back out living on the streets again.

I very much wanted a change. I felt done with Atlanta. My sister was sitting there, telling me that she would help me start my life over in Charleston. That was very appealing. I was deep in addiction. When I really took stock of things, I could see that staying was a mistake. After three years in Atlanta, I needed a change, and it wasn't one that I could make surrounded by drugs and alcohol. I realized that I was ready to go. Here I had a chance to start over somewhere else.

"Okay," I said. "I'll do it. I'll go to Charleston."

Chapter 6

STARTING OVER ... SOMEWHAT

NOTHING, NOWHERE

September 1990

Wadmalaw Island, South Carolina

Moving to Charleston was supposed to give me a new, better life. That would eventually feel true—*eventually*. It did not at first. Kym and her husband didn't even live in Charleston proper. Their house was on Wadmalaw Island, which is surrounded by waterways and creeks. We were at the end of Bear Bluff Road, a good twenty or thirty miles from the city, surrounded by rural farmland and cabin after cabin for miles. This was a far cry from Atlanta and the metal scene. Standing on the dock with my feet down in the water and sand, looking out over the water, I felt like it was the end of the earth.

I needed a job. The resorts were the only game in town for a city kid without an education or any real skills. I cut my hair short and started applying there. Without a car, this was a logistical nightmare. Nothing was within walking distance. I depended on Kym for rides, but she was not always dependable. When she wasn't around, I had no way of getting to the city or the resorts to put in applications.

The dock behind the house overlooked Tidal Water Creek. I sometimes sat out on the dock, tossing pebbles into the water and drinking all day. This was depressing. I regretted leaving Atlanta. I didn't have a job. I didn't have my own place. I was supposed to use my inheritance money to enroll in college, but I quickly dropped all my classes. It felt hard and pointless to take classes without a real goal.

I started to resent my sister for dragging me out there under false pretenses. At the funeral, she had portrayed herself as the more mature sibling, the stable and responsible one. This turned out to be a sham. She was having an affair with another man, a fact she no longer tried to hide. Her boyfriend would come to the house when her husband was away at work.

I wasn't close to Kym's husband, but he was a good guy who was letting me stay in his house. I felt guilty knowing that my sister was running around behind his back. It wasn't my marriage, and I didn't want to get involved. There is no excusing adultery, but Kym had her reasons. She was a city girl who liked to party. Her husband was a country boy from South Carolina. They had gotten married too young, and it was probably doomed to fail from the start. I think Kym felt trapped.

Whatever her reasons, staying in their guest room was not a viable option. This was partly because their marriage was on the rocks but mostly because the boyfriend was into cocaine. They would break out lines on the kitchen table when he came over. I would go line for line with them. I had come to Charleston to get away from drugs but was hanging out with drug dealers and drinking every day. I needed to get out of the house.

THE SUN DANCER

1991

It took me about six months. I used $1,000 of my inheritance money to buy an old beater of a car and landed a bartending job at the resort by lying. My only experience in the service industry was in kitchen jobs and a short stint waiting tables. I had never been behind a bar, but that didn't stop me from claiming otherwise.

The Sun Dancer was a beach bar at the resort. The job consisted mostly of cracking open beers and pouring frozen daiquiris all day long. How hard could it be?

The hiring manager called me out halfway into my first shift. "You've never done this before, have you?"

"No," I confessed.

"That's all right," she said. "You're cute. You can stay."

I stayed in that job for a year. This was my first real taste of the service industry. Prior to the Sun Dancer. Most of my jobs had been as a line cook at chain restaurants. People didn't take much pride in those jobs. The wait staff was usually transient. Everyone would work for a few years until they graduated college or started their real careers. Working at the resort, I started to realize that there was a whole community of people who took the industry seriously. They would come into the bar after work and tell stories. I started to get to know people in the industry. Everyone knew each other. It was like one big extended family, and—slowly at first—I was becoming a part of it.

This was the first time the restaurant saved my life. I truly believe I would be dead had I not found this community of souls—even in the after-work dysfunction, there was unconditional love, which I wanted and needed.

> **I truly believe I would be dead had I not found this community of souls.**

They didn't care who you knew or where you were from. They didn't care about your past. If you showed up for your shifts and worked hard, you were part of the family. This was a new experience for me. I had always felt like the odd man out. My friends had never felt like family. My actual *family* had never felt like family. I had been longing for acceptance my whole life and was finally finding it.

This was all very different from my time in the music scene, where it was all about business. Everyone was always looking to get ahead and get noticed. It could be very superficial and individualistic. In the restaurant industry, we were working *together*. There was no personal glory in waiting tables and pouring drinks. You weren't trying to stand out. You were trying to shore up the team and make the establishment look good. This felt right. Slowly, I started to appreciate being away from that and being among good people who cared about good people.

Unfortunately, things were falling apart with my sister. Her husband wasn't dumb. He caught on to what was going on. Kym would sometimes stay out all evening while I was home with her husband. It was painfully awkward. One day, he asked me point blank whether my sister had a thing going with someone. My silence spoke volumes.

Their marriage entered a terminal decline. Within a year, she left her husband and ran off to Miami with her boyfriend. We stopped talking again. She blamed me for the disintegration of her marriage because I hadn't lied about the affair on her behalf. This caused a big fight, and we had a falling out. She wanted me out of their house.

By that time I was on my feet. I had a car and my job at the Sun Dancer. I met a guy at the watering hole down by the marina who needed a roommate and was able to move out on my own. My new life in Charleston was coming together.

Being away from Atlanta actually helped. In the recovery community, we talk about the ineffectiveness of the "geographical cure." People often move to get away from drugs. This can help shake things up. Getting yourself out of an unsafe environment where drugs are easily accessible and everyone is drinking can help. But there are bars and liquor stores in every city in America. Even small towns have drug dealers. I walked right back into cocaine almost on day one.

Nonetheless, Charleston did give me a fresh start. I had a job. I had a roof over my head. I wasn't crashing on couches and living on the streets. My bills were paid, and there was even a little money in my pocket. I was still drinking almost every night and occasionally using drugs, but less so than before. I had at last some greater sense of normalcy for the first time.

AN UNLIKELY ROMANCE

Around this time, I had one of my first healthy relationships. A woman sat down at my bar one day and introduced herself. She was on Kiawah Island to renovate her parents' beach house while processing her recent divorce.

At thirty-four, she had more than a decade on me. I had just turned twenty-one. Age wasn't our only mismatch. She came from a prominent and wealthy family. She was cultured and sophisticated in ways that were unfamiliar to me. None of this stopped us. She showed up again a few days later. We started dating and fell in love.

It is hard to overstate how healing the relationship was for me. My whole life, I had felt unlovable. This mature, capable, sophisticated woman was proof to the contrary.

The relationship had complications, though. I often felt insecure about being so young and unaccomplished. She seemed so much better than me—how could I not put her up on a pedestal? I didn't understand what she saw in me, which made her love hard to trust. I worried people would think that I was dating her for her money. We eventually moved in together. We lived in a massive historic house in downtown Charleston that was out of my price range. She paid the rent.

None of this bothered me personally. While I'm sure people gossiped about our age and wealth gap, it wasn't an issue for me. I wanted to spend the rest of my life with her and said as much. She wouldn't say it back, though. Her reservations were clear. We split up after about a year and a half. We are still friends. Much later in life, she admitted that she was afraid how her family would react if we had gotten engaged.

I have zero regrets. She exposed me to higher society and showed me how to dress better. She made me, a clueless kid, a little less clueless. She showed me love at a time I believed myself unlovable. I am grateful to her for loving me when I didn't know how to love myself. The relationship was exactly what I needed at the time.

So was my job at the Sun Dancer. I was passionate about bartending. It felt as if everything was coming together. The last ten years had been so bad. Things were finally turning around. For once, I felt hopeful about the future.

One day, late into the fall, I was standing knee deep in the ocean.

The water was cold and the beach empty. I stood there looking out over the Atlantic. A year before, I had been sitting out on the dock behind Kym's house, looking out over the creek and feeling so small and hopeless. This was the opposite feeling. The ocean and sky were so big and beautiful. Life felt so big and beautiful that it was almost too much. I started to tear up.

Chapter 7

FINE DINING AND THE YEARS OF NO CONSEQUENCES

A NEW JOB

1991

Charleston, South Carolina

I was serving drinks at the Sun Dancer one day when some other industry guys came into the bar. The place was packed, they pulled up a few stools, and we got to talking shop while I poured their drinks. They were opening a new restaurant called Magnolias in downtown Charleston. Two of them, Chris Goss and Bernie Smith, watched me hustling behind the bar and chatting it up with the regulars. They must have been impressed, because they offered me a wait job at the new restaurant right there on the spot.

I jumped at the opportunity. This was before my girlfriend and I moved to Charleston. Winters on Kiawah Island were quiet during the off-season. I was getting antsy to be back in a real city. My girl-friend and I had already been talking about moving to Charleston. The job also sounded fantastic.

This was one of my luckiest breaks in the hospitality industry. Magnolias was destined to be the best restaurant in the city upon opening. These were the most coveted wait jobs in the city. I was only twenty-two years old and the least-experienced person on staff. Everyone else had years of experience in fine dining. I had only about a year of bartending experience in a beachside bar and a few line-cook jobs under my belt. Chris and Bernie hired me on personality and potential alone. I was determined not to let them down.

The job was involved, the training intense. We had to know the menu inside and out in minute detail. Learning the dishes on offer wasn't enough. We had to know where the key ingredients were sourced. We had to understand wine pairings. We had to understand presentation and how the dishes fit into the restaurant's overall concept.

These were the early days of enlightened hospitality, popularized by Danny Meyer, which focused on how the delivery of the product makes guests *feel*. We weren't just serving food and drinks. We were creating a unique experience, a novel concept at the time.

Chris, a founding partner, explained the concept to me. I'll never forget it. I was standing at table thirty-six. It was four o'clock on a Thursday afternoon.

"People don't go out to eat," he said. "They go out to have an *experience*. We're here to create that experience."

This was not how restaurants operated in the early 1990s. We were at the vanguard of an industry revolution. Fine dining was a niche sector in the industry. Fine dining wasn't mainstream. No one used words like *foodie* or *gastropub*. Celebrity chefs weren't a thing.

There was no Anthony Bourdain, no Top Chef, no Food Network. All of that was years away.

For me, at twenty-two in 1991, Chris's words were a light-bulb moment. Magnolias awoke a passion in me. I realized that this wasn't just some job. It could be my calling. Lots of people work in restaurants while figuring out what to do with their lives. Not me. I knew right then that this was going to be my career. It was going to be my life. I had found my place, my purpose, and my people. For the first time, I felt like I belonged somewhere.

This was a strange way to feel about the industry in the early 1990s. I was incredibly lucky to get in on the ground floor of what would become a renaissance in elevated dining. I had gone straight from bartending at an oceanside resort in the middle of nowhere to serving at one of the finest restaurants in the country. I never had to sling wings. I had barely even paid my dues in chain restaurants.

I was incredibly lucky to get in on the ground floor of what would become a renaissance in elevated dining.

I pushed myself hard to succeed. I wanted to impress the owners and managers. I wanted the rest of the staff to like me. I wanted the guests to like me. For once, my insecurities and insatiable need to please others and belong was actually an asset.

Sometimes our flaws, when properly channeled, can be our greatest strengths. I was more than a people pleaser. I was driven by a pathological need to be liked. This wasn't always healthy, but it probably made me a better server. I like making people happy, which is what the restaurant industry is all about.

I was good at the job and started being recognized right away. My personality was suited to hospitality. I liked making people happy and sharing in their lives. People were coming in for big date nights, engagements, celebrations, retirements, and other major life events. We got to pop the champagne and celebrate with them. I loved that, and it showed. People could see how passionate I was about the work, the restaurant, and the industry.

MY PLACE, MY PURPOSE, MY PEOPLE

My first high-end restaurant job felt like making it on Broadway. Magnolias exposed me to a whole new world. The wait staff was knowledgeable and sophisticated. Coworkers took me shopping and helped me pick out appropriate clothes. We weren't snobby or pretentious. We just took the job seriously. This was fine dining. We had to dress and act the part.

My tastes became more refined. Most kids in their early twenties are slamming Bud Light and Jell-O shots. We were being treated to hundred-dollar bottles of wine in the back of the restaurant. The restaurant sent us out to Napa Valley to visit wineries. We felt sophisticated. On nights off, we dined at fancy restaurants in order to learn about food and presentation. We treated food and beverage as both science and art. We were always learning. I read books on elevated dining. I was living and breathing fine dining around the clock.

At this level, the restaurant industry feels glamorous. There was a certain grandiosity to working at Magnolias. We booked tables a month in advance, which was uncommon in those days. We took pride in our work. We were *the* Magnolias crew, and in this insular world, that meant something. After work, we would hit the industry hangouts with a swagger in our step. Industry people respected our knowledge and coveted our jobs.

I felt good at something for once. Finding my place in the restaurant business was helping me find my place in the world. I had also found my people and in them a sense of belonging. Staff shared a passion for the work and the experience we were creating. We worked together as an *elite* team. There was no way to do this alone. The work was inherently collaborative. When it was eight o'clock on a Saturday with two hundred people sitting down for dinner, we could pull it off only by working together. We bussed each other's tables, refilled each other's glasses on the way to the kitchen, checked each other's tables, all of us moving a hundred miles an hour.

Working together so closely created an incredibly intimate environment. In the restaurant industry, we interact directly with the entire team in a fluid manner our entire shift. We see each other more than we do our own friends and family. We *become* friends and family. We bond over sweat and stress. Around midnight or so, the kitchen closes, last call comes and goes, and the last tables leave. We close up and head out the door still jacked full of adrenaline. Every single night, we would make a beeline straight for the bar to blow off steam. We'd high-five each other over drinks and trade stories about the eccentric customer who sent their plate back six times and the bottle of wine that slipped between fingers and shattered across table nine.

THE DUALITY OF THE
RESTAURANT INDUSTRY

This lifestyle leads to an unfortunate duality of the hospitality industry. Industry people are some of the most passionate and caring people you will ever meet, but we often fail to take care of ourselves. We work hard, but we party even harder. The late-night Charleston bars stayed open until six o'clock in the morning back then. We closed them down after most shifts. We would stay out all night drinking, sleep till noon, and then roll into work the next day hungover. I was making $1,000 a week in cash, a lot of money at the time for someone my age. After rent and bills, every last cent went to partying.

Industry people are some of the most passionate and caring people you will ever meet, but we often fail to take care of ourselves.

I was lucky to have been hired at Magnolias. But the job and the wonderful career that followed required me to be around alcohol all day, every day. I was already drinking every night. The industry isn't to blame for my addiction. I was probably always destined to be an addict. But moving downtown and becoming enmeshed in the industry caused my drinking to tick up. It felt impossible to say no to drinks after work. Sitting out drinks meant missing out on a key part of the bonding experience. I'm a social animal. I wanted to be around my people.

Not everyone drank as heavily as I did. The industry was why I couldn't say no to drinks, but not being able to say no to the third, fourth, sixth, tenth drink and then lines of cocaine in the bathroom— that was a product of my own personal demons. I had come to Charleston to make a clean break without actually doing anything to get and stay clean. My scenery had changed, but I was still the same me. The geographical cure failed once again. I'd brought all my old problems with me.

I would not talk about my past. I wanted to leave the past in Atlanta. I never went back to visit. My mother and I didn't even talk on the phone. I wanted to keep as much distance between me and that place as possible. I wouldn't even talk about Atlanta. My old life was shameful and embarrassing. I didn't want anyone to know about the homelessness or the drugs. I didn't want people to know about my mother or the things that had happened to me. I wanted that clean break.

I was drinking more than ever. I was taking drugs. I was still seething with resentment for my mother. Despite all my progress, I was still insecure. My life had gotten better, but I couldn't trust that it wouldn't all disappear. I couldn't trust myself not to mess it up. People at the restaurant were showering me with praise. I had the respect of coworkers. But that voice in the back of my head telling me that I wasn't good enough was still there. The same sense of impending doom that had followed me my whole life hadn't gone anywhere. It was dormant at times, but ever present.

Some of these feelings were distortions created by trauma, but they were also rooted in objective reality. I *was* messing up. I was still getting drunk every night. I was using drugs. The duality of the restaurant industry was the duality of my life. I was doing well on the surface, getting good jobs, getting promotions. I was training as a sommelier and exploring my passions in this new industry. My drinking remained problematic. It was just easier to hide. Drinking and drugging were so normalized in the industry that you could abuse alcohol in plain sight without raising an eyebrow. It was easy to pretend that getting smashed every night was normal, because in the industry, it was. No one had a problem with it—not yet. Lots of other people did the same. Drinking wasn't something to be ashamed of—not in this place. Drinking was practically part of the job.

We took a misplaced pride in drinking too much. We would boast about how much we could throw back in a night. No one cared. We could drink whatever we wanted as long as we could still do the job. That was the code. Anything goes as long as you get your butt in to work the next morning and do the job with pride. And I did. I would work doubles six days a week and always went out drinking afterward, caught four hours of fitful sleep, and was back to work the next day.

I was able to rationalize all of this away because drinking was still fun at this point. It was helping me bond with my coworkers. There was nothing but upside. In the recovery community, we call these the "years of no consequence." I wasn't overdosing or losing jobs. Everyone around me was drinking heavily, and they were all fine. No one was getting DUIs or wrecking cars. It was a carefree time. I was happy for the first time in my life. We were getting messed up, but it didn't lead me to despair. The darkness of my youth had parted a little, sometimes. My bills and rent were getting paid, even if it meant pulling extra shifts because I had spent all my money partying. I felt more stable. I had a tribe and a sense of purpose. Despite the warning signs, I was happier than I had ever been.

When that old sense of impending doom did surface, it was easy to drown it out with alcohol and hard work. The alcohol still worked, and it wasn't causing me major problems—not yet. I wasn't physically addicted. I didn't wake up with the shakes. I didn't have to drink to function. I could stay out at the bar all night and shrug off the hangover with a pot of coffee.

BLOSSOM CAFÉ

1992–1995

Magnolias did so well that the owners opened a second restaurant, the Blossom Café, next door. The new restaurant was a Mediterranean bistro. They hired one of the waiters at Magnolias as the new GM. By this time, I had a few years of experience under my belt and had received a whole lot of praise and acknowledgment. Recognizing my passion for service, they had made me one of the service trainers. I was excited to be working in a new environment, serving cuisine that was new to Charleston and helping to train the staff. I led classes on table service and the menu, which gave me the opportunity to share my passion for hospitality with others.

The lead-up to the grand opening was incredibly exciting and incredibly stressful. The success of Magnolias created a lot of buzz around the new restaurant before we even opened the doors. Blossom catered to a younger crowd. The bar and kitchen stayed open late. We skipped the tablecloths. The speakers were pumping Counting Crows and Dave Matthews Band.

Opening a new restaurant is a bonding experience. It is the ultimate roller-coaster ride. Scared to death, nervous and anxious, and then *bam*! The adrenaline hits on opening night, and you want to do it all over again. It is a sublime sickness like no other. I became very close to the crew. The hours leading up to the grand opening were long. Some of us were putting in seventy hours a week. We became known as the Blossom Boys' Club. We were always together. If we weren't working, we were partying like there was no tomorrow. We all had Mondays off and would rent a boat and spend the whole day drinking out on the water. We called it "motorboat Mondays."

For my twenty-fifth birthday, we picked up a few cases of wine and rented a lake house. Someone brought cocaine. We got totally smashed, but it was wrapped up in the veneer of work. We sampled wines—whole bottles of them at a time. We were comparing styles and vintages. I was out on the water, the boat rocking in the ocean waves, and everything felt perfect. I loved these people. I loved this business. I wanted to do exactly this for the rest of my life.

CANOE

1995

Atlanta, Georgia

Not long after the weekend at the lake, David LeBoutillier recruited some of us to help open a new restaurant in Atlanta called Canoe. He had been the director of operations at Magnolias and Blossom. He brought several of us with him to the new restaurant. My roommate was brought on as a line cook. They tapped me to be the head trainer and eventually the wine director. We all quit our jobs and moved to Atlanta together.

This was not a decision I made lightly. Going back to Atlanta made me anxious. The darkest times of my life had been in Atlanta. I associated the city with homelessness, jail, and drugs. Coming to Charleston had been my escape. I was still drinking and taking drugs, but my life was better on balance. Part of me feared getting sucked back into that old life.

But this was a great career opportunity. There was a lot of hype around the restaurant, even more than there had been around Blossom. The Olympics were coming to Atlanta the following year, which was driving a lot of interest in the city and buzz around the restaurant scene. The concept for the restaurant was great. A famous chef was helping with the opening. They were offering me a leadership position. It felt like the next step in my career.

The restaurant was another hit. We served five hundred guests on opening night. I had never worked in such a busy fine-dining establishment. We were doing double the sales of Blossom and Magnolias right out of the gate. The press was huge. The restaurant was nominated for a James Beard Award. We appeared on the cover of *Wine Spectator* magazine. It was dizzying.

This was a strange time for me. The duality of the restaurant industry—that it contains some of the best, most caring people who cannot always take care of themselves—was playing out all around me and in my own life. My personal journey was a microcosm of the greater industry. I had gotten into fine dining just as the industry was getting bigger. I had front-row seats to both the industry revolution and the dark underbelly beneath.

At Canoe, we were all deep into drugs and alcohol. On opening night, a manager pulled me and a couple of chefs into a back closet and laid out a rail of cocaine for each of us. I hadn't done cocaine since the night at the lake house. It probably helped that cocaine had fallen somewhat out of fashion, making it hard to come by in Charleston. Everyone was into ecstasy and mushrooms, which had the benefit of not causing me to binge on alcohol. But back in Atlanta, I now had access to cocaine and plenty of it.

On my journey through addiction, this was a fork in the road. It wasn't just that line of cocaine. It was my pattern of use. It was working at Canoe with other leaders who were also doing cocaine. We drank nonstop—*at* work and afterward. It never stopped. I barely slept. Canoe served lunch, too, which meant that we often closed late and had to be up early for work the next day. Where before I was getting four hours of sleep a night, now I was getting none. I would get so high on cocaine that I would sometimes guzzle a bottle of vodka at four in the morning just to pass out for a few hours before my lunch shift. Sometimes I was so coked up that even this didn't work. There is nothing more soul crushing than lying awake in bed, tweaked out, as the sun comes up before your shift that day.

This is also when I started getting in trouble while drinking. Security threw me out of a bar one night. I was almost blackout drunk and started shouting at the bouncer. I was being a total drunken asshole. I taunted him about making more money as a waiter than he did as a bouncer. I did not know that he was an off-duty cop. He had me arrested out in the parking lot, and I spent the night in jail.

Working at Canoe taught me much, but I also have deep regrets about some of my behavior there. Somewhere during this time, my drinking crossed over into actual, physical addiction. Morning anxiety gave way to morning shakes. The only way to keep my hands from trembling at work was to drink before going in. Drinking was no longer something I wanted to do. It was something I had to do. I stopped being fun. Alcohol was the master now, me the slave. The years of no consequences had drawn to a close.

Drinking was no longer something I wanted to do. It was something I had to do.

Chapter 8

A TASTE OF ENTREPRENEURSHIP

THE COMPANY THAT NEVER WAS

1996

Savannah, Georgia

My time in Atlanta was short lived. I had followed David LeBoutillier from Charleston to Atlanta to open Canoe. About two years later, I left for Savannah to start a restaurant of my own, along with my mentors-turned-partners.

Right away, there were problems with the money. The investors were always *just about* to cut a check, but there was always some excuse for why the money didn't come through. Eventually, it became clear that we were dealing with a crook. We weren't the happiest of partners. There was a lot of tension between us, and we were all blaming each other for the restaurant failing to materialize.

In reality, there was plenty of blame to go around. I was getting drunk every day, just trying to stay positive. Lots of us were getting messed up all the time. We sometimes didn't treat each other right. As with so many partnerships in our industry, the tension between us was the result of passionate, creative souls with good intentions falling short of expectations due to addiction and mental health issues.

Since the restaurant was on hold, we started a consulting company. Our clients hired us to help open and run *their* restaurants. We did conception and design. We worked on menus. We tasted the food and the wines. We judged palate and presentation. We worked with interior designers to help balance aesthetics with functionality. We designed both kitchens and dining rooms. We recruited and trained staff.

> *This was a learning experience, which for me was the most valuable thing about those years.*

This was a learning experience, which for me was the most valuable thing about those years. I found that I loved opening restaurants. It is an involved process that happens while the clock is ticking. The doors need to be open before the owners run out of money. Opening night is critical for a fine-dining establishment. You want to get people talking and saying good things. The restaurant has to run seamlessly from day one. The invitations have to go out to the right people well in advance in order to make a big splash on the debut. The lead-up is incredibly stressful. Critics are there—local and national trendsetters, big names in the community.

We hadn't come to Savannah to be consultants, but at least we were landing legitimate clients and getting paid—a little. These were lean years. We were always chasing checks and new clients. The runaround never ceased. The hustle was constant. Despite bringing in a few big consulting deals a year, we still lived hand to mouth.

My main job was to train staff for our clients. Teaching hospitality has always been fun and rewarding for me. It makes me feel good at the job and knowledgeable about the industry. It was validating to walk into a new restaurant where everyone treated me as the authority.

While the work was rewarding, I was getting frustrated. I was working sixteen hours a day with very little to show for it. I had come to Savannah to learn about opening restaurants and running a business under my mentors, but it wasn't really going as planned. Much of the blame can be laid at my own feet, as I was deep into alcohol and drugs.

Eventually, I got restless. I was making only $2,000 a month as a consultant. At Canoe, I had been averaging $60,000 a year between wages and tips. I was making a third of that now and had to chase after checks to get paid. I was starting to regret my decision to come to Savannah.

To leave Atlanta, I'd had to break things off with my future wife (now ex-wife). We'd met opening night at Canoe. She was on the wait staff. Our relationship had problems right from the start. She had grown up in a volatile household and was dealing with traumas of her own. She was similar to my mother in that she dealt with fear by tightening her grip on things. This made her controlling and rigid at times. She was a planner and couldn't tolerate deviations from the plan. It tortured her not to feel in charge.

This really didn't work for me, an alcoholic. She tried to control every aspect of my life. When we got more serious, she controlled everything. She managed the checking account. She monitored and paid the bills. I couldn't be trusted with any of it. Everything was in her name. She always wanted to know where I was and what I was doing. She didn't like me spending time with my friends, whom she blamed for my drug and alcohol problems, and they didn't like her either.

Her controlling nature conflicted with my off-the-cuff approach to life, but I was too much of a mess to handle things on my own. That became the narrative of our relationship. Even though I was three years older, she was the responsible adult. I was the fuckup. There was some truth to this narrative, but it was an unhealthy dynamic. I resented feeling controlled and infantilized. I especially hated when she tried to place limits on my alcohol and drug use. She drank socially and didn't mind marijuana—what she called "natural" stuff—but didn't like me using cocaine or getting drunk.

While she was right about my drinking and drug use, we also weren't right for each other. We were polar opposites in so many ways. She was going to school to be a teacher. I was a high school dropout. She was a straight-laced, small-town girl. I had been a city kid and was still into rock music and drugs. She dressed conservatively. My hair had grown back out, and I kept it pulled into a ponytail. She was rigid. I was easygoing.

The only reason we had worked at all was because of our codependency. She needed someone to nurture and control. I was her fixer-upper project. I needed someone to control my worst impulses and habits. I don't know that we would have lasted as long together absent my addiction. Addiction kept me in a constant state of chaos. She helped me feel more stable. The whole thing didn't really make any sense—not in a good way.

I told her as much when making the decision to move to Savannah. "We need to be honest," I said, cutting things off before leaving. "We both know this isn't working."

We were broken up for about six months. I moved. Then one day, she showed up in Savannah unannounced.

"I want to try to make this work," she said. "I love you."

Though still unsure we belonged together, I was touched that she had driven all the way from Atlanta. By this time, I was feeling more and more out of control. The geographical cure had failed again. My drinking and drugging were getting really bad, and there was no one to check me at all. Between consulting gigs, there was nothing to do but drink and get high. The "company" was a complete joke, and I felt lost on my own. She had been my life raft, and I wasn't keeping my head above water on my own. So we got back together.

Of course, she couldn't fix my problems. The company was a train wreck. I was working like a dog. Savannah was not a good place for me. It's a strange place with a dark, gothic feel, not unlike New Orleans. It was like stumbling onto the set of some Tennessee Williams production. Locals will tell you the city was built on Indian burial grounds. The whole town felt eerie at times, especially when I was messed up on drugs and alcohol, which was most of the time. The town seemed to mirror the darkness in my heart. It was becoming clear that it was time to go.

OPENING THE PENINSULA GRILL

1997

Charleston, South Carolina

When a new client hired us to help open a restaurant in Charleston, I was relieved to be getting out of Savannah. This was the Peninsula Grill, where I would go on to be the GM. This was when I met Hank Holliday, the owner, and Bob Carter, one of the chefs—the two men who would later stage my intervention and send me back to rehab. They were brilliant people. Hank was a savvy businessman. Bob was a creative genius. He was the kind of chef who visited tables in the dining room to make sure that the food was coming out properly. The guests loved him. He was not only talented but passionate and charismatic.

The concept behind the restaurant was to elevate Southern cooking into the world of fine dining. This hadn't really been done before, not at this scale, not in such a grand way. We served caviar alongside fried green tomatoes instead of toast points. No other restaurant in the country was putting up velvet walls and serving country cooking. There was nowhere else you could get served grits alongside Dom Pérignon. We had the longest wine list of any restaurant in the city. The cellar was stocked with $500 bottles of wine.

No other restaurant in the country was putting up velvet walls and serving country cooking.

This was all a calculated risk. We didn't know whether or not people would balk at the prices. Opening a restaurant is an emotional roller coaster. Buckets of blood, sweat, and tears are spilled up front. Concepting and construction precede opening. You never know what will or won't work, not for sure. It's always a risk—and the best restaurants take the greatest risks. And there's a lot of money on the line. Many new restaurants fail. But when everything clicks and the public connects, there's just no greater feeling. You finally get to see the concept come to life. It's incredibly stressful but oh so rewarding when the concept works. It's only then, when the ride is over, that you can really appreciate all the twists and turns and scares you had along the way. And then you immediately want to do it all again.

The restaurant was an immediate hit. We brought national attention to the Charleston restaurant scene at a time when fine dining was becoming mainstream. We got good write-ups in the industry magazines. Glossies like *Esquire* showered us with praise. The restaurant made and even topped many of the "best of" lists that year.

Our consulting contract was only for six months, but once it was up and the restaurant was open, I didn't want to leave. My friends were all there. My girlfriend was there. I liked being back in Charleston and didn't want to go back to Savannah. The company wasn't going anywhere. From the outside, we looked successful. We had helped open half a dozen restaurants for our clients. (Four of them are still open and profitable twenty years later.) But the money wasn't trickling down. After almost two years, I was still barely getting by and we weren't any closer to opening our own restaurant. It had become abundantly clear that we never would.

I quit the consulting company and stayed in Charleston. The Peninsula Grill hired me to wait tables. It felt like a step backward in my career, but I felt burned out and needed a break. My personal life was in shambles. I was drinking way too much. I needed a hard reset, and moving to Charleston had helped the first time—for a little while. I thought maybe it would again. I was going to try the geographical cure again.

Chapter 9

A DOWNWARD SPIRAL

A TROUBLED MARRIAGE

1999

Charleston, South Carolina

I t should come as no surprise that moving back to Charleston did not fix my life. I was doing cocaine all the time. My drinking got worse. I was physically addicted to alcohol and needed it to get through the day.

Hiding all of this from my girlfriend was not easy, especially after we got engaged and then married, as we now lived together. I proposed to her on Miami Beach in the middle of a mushroom trip. We got married shortly thereafter. I wanted to make the relationship work. I walked down the aisle certain that we would find a way. Our friends and family had their doubts, I later learned, but at the time I really believed we could be good for each other.

All the available evidence suggested otherwise. I may have *wanted* to make things work, but my behavior didn't align with my desires. I was getting messed up all the time. I was lying to her about my drinking and using. Sometimes, too pissed to show my face at the house, I would stay out all night and go back to work without sleeping.

I had more run-ins with the law. I was out drinking at a bar after one of my shifts when I saw my friend Chris fall out of his 1970 Bronco. He couldn't even get the key in the ignition much less drive in a straight line, but he still refused a cab. He hated cabs. I offered to drive him home. I had been drinking too but wasn't nearly as trashed. He scooted over into the passenger seat, and I got in.

The Bronco was heavy in the back and prone to fishtailing. We were crossing a bridge to get to the island where Chris lived when the car started to sway. When I swerved to straighten out the car, blue lights started swirling in the rearview mirror.

"Oh, shit," Chris said. "I've got cocaine on me."

The cops gave me a Breathalyzer. When I blew over the limit, they cuffed me and put me in the back of the squad car. I went to jail on a DUI charge. Chris got a ride home with the police with a baggie of cocaine in his pocket.

My wife was furious when she came to bail me out. It wasn't just the DUI. It was everything. We were fighting all the time. We were still newlyweds, but she was already at the end of her rope. She had every right to be angry. I was still lying and hiding things. It wasn't just drugs either. I had stayed out high on ecstasy one night and ended up cheating on her. I had lost my wedding ring in the process. I am obviously not proud of any of this. My behavior was abhorrent, and there was no good excuse.

As bad as things were, she was still trying to make the relationship work. I was too, in a way, but my addiction prevented me from being a good husband.

THE RITZ-CARLTON

2000

St. Louis, Missouri

We left Charleston briefly when I got a job offer from the Ritz-Carlton, which hired me to be the wine director for a resort in St. Louis. They were building a wine cellar with a private dining room inside. This was a major project. They stocked twelve hundred bottles of wine worth more than $1 million down there. I bought wines and managed the collection. I was excited. This was a chance to teach people about wine. I was often out on the floor, opening wines and talking to customers. I even taught classes on wine.

After my stint waiting tables again, this seemed like a solid step forward in my career. But the odd duality of my life was still true. My career was rising, but my personal life continued to spiral downward as my addictions worsened. I was drinking more than ever. Within six weeks of moving to St. Louis, I got another DUI.

By this point, I recognized my drinking as a major problem. I accepted that there was nothing normal about my drinking and took steps to cut back. It was a struggle. My wife tried to be supportive. We enrolled in a twelve-week fitness program together. I was able to cut back on alcohol and even lost some weight. Our relationship improved. But it didn't stick. It never did. My drinking eventually crept back up. I felt powerless to be better.

That's not an excuse. I take responsibility for my actions. It was always my choice to drink. But it didn't *feel* like a choice. I couldn't control my addiction any more than my wife could control me.

Every week it seemed I received another big wake-up call to quit drinking entirely. Driving home drunk one night, I swerved into construction pylons on the side of the highway. The car lurched to a halt with a violent crunch of metal, plastic, and sand. I got out and did a walk around the car, stumbling. It wasn't totaled, but one of the tires was flat, and I was too drunk to replace it with the doughnut in the trunk. A passing car slowed to ask if I was okay. Without thinking, I jumped into the back seat and asked for a ride home. I was too wasted to drive and definitely too wasted to wait for the cops to show up.

The accident was traumatizing. I could have killed someone. I was afraid to tell my wife what happened but had no choice. We shared the one car, and she would have no way to get to class or work. She was so angry that she lost her cool. She punched me with all of her might, right in the face. While this kind of violence is never okay, it was easy to empathize with her. She wasn't a violent person. Our relationship was just dysfunctional. I was ruining her life. It wasn't just the car. It was everything.

Shortly after the accident, I got a phone call from the Peninsula Grill. The general manager was leaving. They wanted me to come run the restaurant. This was another big step up for my career. The job came with a salary and a 10 percent share of profits. I was going to be making well into the six figures for the first time. More importantly, I was going to be running an amazing restaurant that I had helped design and open.

Leaving Missouri was as much of a relief as leaving Savannah had been. I was going to try the geographical cure one more time. In my mind, everything was going to be different when we got back to Charleston. Though pure delusion, I had renewed optimism. It wasn't going to be like last time. This was a good job running a great restaurant. This was going to be my restaurant, and the long hours were just what I needed to quit drinking so much. The more I was working, the less time I would have to drink, I told myself, ignoring my tendency to drink at work.

My wife had mixed feelings about moving back to Charleston. She was excited about the job opportunity, and Missouri had left a bad taste in her mouth. I was getting DUIs and losing cars. I had cheated on her. Everything was terrible. But she was also worried about me being back around my old friends. She didn't share my optimism—with good reason—but she probably also hoped the geographical cure would work. Nothing else seemed to.

OLD BEGINNINGS

2001

Charleston, South Carolina

Of course, Charleston wasn't any better this time. I was running the store, but my drinking never slowed down. It got worse. My cocaine use got worse. I was up all night, coked up and drinking. My mornings started with liquor to stave off the shakes, and my days ended with liquor to knock myself out. I would have an eye-opener or two in the shower before work and the rest of the bottle when I got home from the bar.

I was drinking around the clock out of necessity. I would sneak drinks in the morning. I would sneak drinks at work. I drank on lunch break, on the way home, in the bathroom, in my office in the back. There was always alcohol within reach. I was stealing bottles from the wine cellar and taking shots of Grand Marnier behind the service bar. If I wasn't asleep—and I barely slept—I was drinking.

There was always some excuse not to quit. I told myself that as the restaurant's wine buyer, I *had* to drink wine. I bargained with myself, saying I would stick to wine, but I never stuck just to wine.

A few glasses in and I would be phoning the cocaine dealer. A few lines of coke and moderation went out the window. I would be up drinking all night long.

I justified my drinking by pointing to much success at work. The restaurant was doing well. The numbers were great. I was getting praise for growing the business. Everyone was happy, and everything was great—until they weren't and it wasn't. Eventually, the duality of my life started to break down. I was no longer maintaining my career while my personal life crumbled. They were now both falling apart.

I was no longer maintaining my career while my personal life crumbled. They were now both falling apart.

Things with my wife deteriorated rapidly. The fights started back up right away. She was working at a different restaurant. She had finished her teaching degree but only lasted nine months on the job. She liked being in the classroom but not the red tape. When the school year ended, she had resigned and gone back to waiting tables. She no longer joined us for drinks after her shifts ended, though. She didn't want to watch me drink our marriage away. So I went out alone, sometimes coming home late, sometimes not at all. I broke every promise I ever made to her.

If you have never stayed drunk around the clock, you can't really appreciate how you start to lose touch with reality. The whole year was a blur. I barely remember anything. The 9/11 terrorist attacks happened, and I have only hazy memories of it. Bob, the chef, called me that morning and told me to shake off my hangover and turn on the TV—something big had happened. Even that barely registered. I had become a husk of a person.

This brings me back to where I started this story. I moved back to

Charleston in February. By October, my wife had left. By November, I was headed back to rehab again.

Chapter 10

THE LONG ROAD
TO RECOVERY

THE PAVILION

November 2001–December 2001

Asheville, North Carolina

This was my third stab at rehab. I was thirty-two years old. The program was thirty days and started at the beginning of every month. When Bob, the chef, drove me home to pack my bags and dropped me off at the center, there were still two weeks until the next program started. They were kind enough to let me hang around until the others arrived. I was already detoxed and couldn't be trusted to be on my own.

I had a good idea of what to expect: group therapy, the treatment of addiction as a disease, the Twelve Steps, the Big Book. I had tried it all before. It hadn't worked then, and there was no reason to believe it would be different this time around. Not counting the last few

103

weeks, in which I had somehow managed to detox on my own, I had been drinking almost every day of my adult life. I had lost the better part of a decade to around-the-clock heavy drinking. I felt constitutionally incapable of sobriety. My hopelessness and despair were ever present even as we drove to rehab.

There is a passage in the Twelve Steps literature that acknowledges that some people fail to ever get sober because they are constitutionally incapable of being honest with themselves. The passage refers to people with sociopathic personality disorders, but that's not how I read it. I thought they were talking about *me*. That is exactly how I felt: incapable of being honest with myself and fundamentally unfit for sobriety.

> *That is exactly how I felt: incapable of being honest with myself and fundamentally unfit for sobriety.*

But I was open to trying. I had prayed to be put somewhere where alcohol was inaccessible. My prayer was answered. This was no accident. It was divine intervention. God had answered my prayer, and I was going to do him a solid and at least try to get sober. I wasn't optimistic about my prospects. But I did have a lot of hope. Maybe it wouldn't work, but I wanted it to and was going to try, no matter the likely outcome.

The rehab was called the Pavilion, a scenic retreat in Asheville, North Carolina. It was the perfect environment for reconnecting with my inner self. In the morning, we did yoga with the sun coming up over the mountains. We went for walks around the lake in the afternoon. I felt grounded in the moment. I had no responsibilities or duties except to be there and work on getting better. My everyday worries were put on pause. I didn't have to worry about DUIs or trouble at work. I didn't have to think about my marriage or the restaurant. My head was clear for the first time maybe ever. I could focus on my body and my mind and just exist in the world. This made the benefits of sobriety crystal clear. I hadn't known such peace and quiet for a long time. And for the first time in a long time, I had a small sliver of hope that things could be different.

The program was not a superficial retreat. This was no resort. The staff was caring and supportive. The people in my group were committed to healing. We bared everything. It was brutal at times. We shined a light on the dark corners of our pasts, looking for the root sources of our angers and resentments. We were searching for the traumas that had led us there. Talking was not optional. Canned responses were not allowed. We held each other accountable and asked questions that forced one another to dig ever deeper. We were honest with each other in order to be honest with ourselves. We stared down the scariest, ugliest parts of ourselves to face the hard truth about our lives and found self-love and acceptance in the most painful of moments.

Letting go of anger and resentment is key to the recovery process. Clinging to resentment is like drinking poison and hoping the other person gets sick. My resentments traced back to my mother. But my resentment wasn't hurting her—it was only hurting me. It was literally killing me. I had to let go of all of that to find peace.

I worked through much of this in group. We did anger regression treatments. They handed us a paddle and a pillow and we literally beat our anger out in order to clear our heads before group. Then we would talk. I talked about my family, how my father had died young and how my mother had treated me as a child. My mother and her choices were shadows hanging over my life. They were killing me. In order to get sober, I had to let go of that anger. I wasn't quite ready to forgive, though I tried, but I was able to make peace with the past. I was able to start accepting the things that had happened to me and take responsibility for what I had done to myself and others.

The process was more than I ever could have hoped for. There were a lot of tears and a lot of healing. Starting to let go of all that anger felt cathartic. I formed lifelong bonds with people in the group, many of whom I have stayed in touch with to today. What we went through together was a sacred experience I will never forget or take for granted. Once again, someone had shown me love when I couldn't love myself. I will forever be grateful.

The six weeks passed quickly. I didn't want it to end. I didn't want to go home or back to work. Thinking about it gave me anxiety. Staying sober in an inpatient program isn't easy, but in many ways it is passive. You are separated from your daily life, which is absolutely necessary as a reset, but eventually you have to face sobriety in the real world.

BACK HOME

2001

Charleston, South Carolina

I caught a ride home from rehab with another patient, a dentist from Charleston. He dropped me off in front of my house. I stood there for a long while before going inside and sitting down on the couch. My wife was long gone. Without alcohol to keep me company, the house felt empty and dead. I didn't know what to do with myself or what came next. The prospect of going back to work and being around alcohol terrified me, but I didn't know what else to do.

I called Hank. We hadn't talked since the intervention. Despite giving me the money for rehab, he was very upset with me. He made it clear that I had let them down. I had been stealing alcohol from the stock and embarrassing the restaurant with my behavior. They had been forced to pick up my slack and run the store without me for the last six weeks. He took a tough love approach.

"Listen, you're welcome back, but you've let a lot of people down," Hank said. "And you need to understand that."

I had messed up big time. They weren't going to throw me a parade for making it through rehab. I was going to have to earn their trust back—and that was going to take time and a lot of effort. It would be a good minute before Hank and I could smile and laugh together again. I was in a probationary period. They wanted me to do ninety days of follow-up outpatient treatment. They were going to dock my pay to cover the cost of rehab. That was fine with me. I was desperate and would have done anything he asked.

He told me to take the rest of the week off to get reacclimated to being home. He probably didn't want to let me back in the restaurant if I was just going to go straight back to the bottle. I was relieved to not have to go back to work yet, but home wasn't much better. I didn't know how to make it through a day without drinking.

Taking another week off also meant going another week without income. My bank account was already overdrawn by $600. The food in the fridge had all gone bad. I didn't know how I was going to feed myself. I called my sister and asked to borrow money for groceries and gas. She loaned me the money.

That first day in the house alone was terrible. The idea of leaving the house left me petrified. I didn't want to walk by liquor stores or corner stores where I used to get booze. I was afraid of running into my drinking buddies, which were basically all of my friends. I stayed inside and didn't talk to anyone.

The next day, a Sunday afternoon, my best friend at the time called. He had heard that they'd let me out. He invited me out to the bar.

"You're not an alcoholic," he said. "Hank's making a big deal out of nothing. You're fine."

Drinking buddies often react this way when you get sober. They don't want to admit that there was anything wrong with your behavior because it casts a light on *their* behavior. We used to drink together all the time. We would go drink for drink all night long. Acknowledging my drinking problem was tantamount to admitting he had one as well.

I turned down the invitation and told him I wanted to stay sober. We hung up the phone. The phone call shook me. I realized this was just the beginning. This was not rehab. This was life. I was going to be faced with constant temptation—forever. I needed to get support, or my sobriety wasn't going to last. I thumbed through the yellow pages and found a hotline for people trying to quit drinking. I dialed the number and listened to the phone ring and then pick up. The person on the other end of the line helped me find a Twelve Steps group within walking distance. I went to my first meeting that evening.

There were three or four other guys there when I showed up. One of them looked homeless. He wasn't wearing shoes. Half of his teeth had rotted out, but he had a kind smile that lit up the room. He introduced himself and welcomed me to the group. I could feel relief wash over me like a wave. I was so glad to be back in a group support setting. I realized that I didn't have to stay home alone. There were people willing to support me in my sobriety. I decided then and there to go to meetings every day.

Twelve Steps meetings became my safe place. My house wasn't safe. There was no one to stop me from going out for alcohol. The restaurant certainly wasn't going to be safe. Most of the people there were drinking or using. Even the chef who drove me to rehab was still doing cocaine and drinking at work. Industry people were some of the most important people in my life—they were my tribe—but at that moment I needed a tribe of people who wanted to stay sober. I found that at Twelve Steps meetings.

In the early days of my sobriety, I sometimes went to meetings three times a day. I found a sponsor, Sheldon Weinstein, who became the most important male figure in my life since losing my father and grandfather. My father had given me life. I didn't know it yet, but Sheldon was going to save my life.

On the surface, we were polar opposites. I was an extrovert and open with my feelings. Sheldon was stoic. I was gentle and emotional. He could be a crusty old bastard. Though only in his forties at the time, he seemed much older. He was far more rigid than I was.

Sheldon wasn't always what I wanted, but he was definitely what I needed. He was what we call a "Big Book thumper" in the recovery community. These are older guys in the recovery community who do everything by the book. They treat the Twelve Steps as gospel. He would give what felt like fire-and-brimstone talks. "We're gonna get sober or die trying!"

We started meeting every Tuesday at Starbucks. When I was ten minutes late once, he left without warning. He scolded me later. "I'm coming to work with you," he said. "The least you can do is show up. When you were drinking, you didn't honor your word. It's time you learn to." Though annoyed at first, I later realized that he was trying to teach me integrity. He was teaching me to be a man of my word. Being ten minutes late might seem like a small matter, but staying true to your word is not how addicts operate. This was a basic life lesson about how to live as a member of society.

And that's what he was ultimately teaching me: how to be a functional person again.

LEARNING TO WORK SOBER

As the week wore on, I got more and more anxious about returning to work. Working at the restaurant seemed incompatible with sobriety. Everyone would want to go out for drinks after close. Was I strong enough to decline? It seemed I might have to leave the industry. My entire life had revolved around alcohol and restaurants—I wasn't ready to walk away from both. I also didn't have any other skills or experience outside of hospitality. I had no money. My housing was paid for by the restaurant. They had just laid down $35,000 to put me through rehab. I couldn't walk away now.

My first shift back was the following Saturday night, exactly one week after leaving rehab. My hands were shaking, and for once it had nothing to do with alcohol. I was scared and embarrassed to show my face at the restaurant. They all knew what had happened. I had let the whole team down and embarrassed myself. How could I walk in now and lead with any authority?

We started each night with a preshift lineup. My skin was crawling. My heart was pounding a mile a minute. I was so scared someone was going to bring up rehab. But they didn't. They didn't ask prying questions. They just said they were glad to have me back. Just like any other day, we went over the daily specials on the menu and got to work. They had accepted me back in without any judgment. I was touched. It was a gift to be in such a supportive community.

The restaurant opened for dinner, and we started serving drinks. I tried to stay far away from the bar, but early into the evening, a server handed me a bottle of wine and asked me to take it to table twenty-five. This was totally normal. We were a team. We helped each other stay out of the weeds. I was the GM, but I was still part of the team. I carried the bottle across the restaurant, my body literally trembling. I didn't want to open the bottle. The smell of wine would hit my nose, and that would be it. I would break down and start drinking in the back, I was sure of it.

Approaching the table, I lost my nerve. I couldn't do it. I had to get away. I handed the bottle off to someone else and left right in the middle of the dinner rush. The restaurant is in a small hotel. I took the elevator up to the roof for a few minutes of solitude. I needed to collect myself. I stood on the roof, trying to control my breathing. I was almost gasping for air.

"God, I can't do this," I said aloud. I really believed it. I was going to have to quit—not just my job but the whole industry.

And just then, as if my prayer were being answered, one word entered my heart: *surrender.* Call it God; call it the still, small voice; call it the universe; call it whatever you prefer—but it was a calming presence. It wasn't a vision. There was no shining light, no burning bush, no angels or anything like that. Just a simple word. *Surrender.*

> *And just then, as if my prayer were being answered, one word entered my heart: surrender.*

And I did. My body stopped shaking. Sweat stopped pouring from my forehead. I felt a sense of calm and well-being. Suddenly, I knew that somehow this was all part of the plan, part of the process, and I was going to get through the shift just as surely as I had gotten through the last week at home, the last six weeks at rehab, the three weeks of detoxing before that. I realized that I hadn't gone through the hell of withdrawal, six weeks of rehab, and meetings every day since to start drinking now. Of course I wasn't going to drink now. I didn't even want a drink. I was just scared of *wanting* to want a drink. But there was no reason to be scared. I just had to surrender. I just had to *let go* of the past. I didn't need to fear the restaurant. This was right where I was supposed to be.

I went back downstairs feeling in control. I wasn't worried anymore. I finished my shift, closed down the restaurant, and went home to bed instead of to the bar. I had made it through the first day.

The next morning, I told Sheldon about what had happened with the bottle of wine. We were supposed to talk every day for the first year. We met in person on Tuesdays. He had me reading books and doing homework. Every other day, if we didn't see each other at a meeting, I would give him a call. I explained how scary it had been to go back to the restaurant. Despite the spiritual experience on the roof, I still didn't think working in the industry was conducive to my sobriety.

"Steve, if you're willing to do the work, you can do anything you want in life," he said. "Getting sober is about having more of a life, not less of one."

Addicts often stay addicts out of fear of the unknown. Giving up drinking feels like giving up your whole life. We worry about losing friends. This is especially true in the restaurant community. Drinking was so tied to my sense of community and camaraderie that it was impossible to imagine giving up one without giving up the other. Going for drinks after work was how we bonded with each other. Giving up drinking felt like giving up those bonds.

There is some truth to these fears. Getting sober often means disconnecting and learning new habits. It can mean giving up old relationships as you build a new life in sobriety. But I eventually came to realize that giving up alcohol didn't have to mean giving up my community. It is possible to go out with coworkers and not drink. People do it all the time. The alcohol and the camaraderie are *not* one and the same. You can have one without the other.

In fact, to Sheldon's point, you can have *more* of everything when you quit abusing alcohol. When we first get sober, addicts are very focused on what we cannot do anymore. We bemoan not being able to have a bottle of wine with dinner or drinks after work. This fades with time. I don't wake up every morning dreading another day without alcohol. Freed from the chains of addiction, you are able to do more,

> *Freed from the chains of addiction, you are able to do more, not less.*

not less. Take away the blackouts and hangovers, the broken promises and the dreams deferred, and you have more time and energy to build the life you actually want.

Framing your life in terms of what you can't do is like looking at a negative and thinking it's the photograph. With time, we begin to reframe. My first day back at work "without" a drink was also my first sober day of work in years. That was a major milestone. I was relearning how to be at work sober.

Sobriety is a series of these kinds of firsts. In the recovery community, we celebrate the first day of sobriety, the first week, the first month, the first year. These milestones are hard earned, but so are the less celebrated ones. There are so many little firsts that surprise you. My first day back at work was just one of them. The first time I boarded an airplane without ordering a Bloody Mary required relearning how to fly. Six months into sobriety, I took a road trip to Charlotte. It was my first long-distance drive without smoking pot. The first time I had sex sober felt like being in high school again. My emotions no longer numb, these simple pleasures would bloom into small moments of gratitude. Even mundane tasks like paying the bills and balancing a checkbook—things that my wife had handled before—took on new meaning. I was relearning how to live.

Real life is hard. Once you stop spending all your time drinking or using, you have to actually fill the days with something else. You have to learn to function as a member of society. That is the real recovery. In meetings, we don't just talk about not drinking or not using. We talk about all facets of life. It's about learning to live a better life. Not drinking, not drugging—those are just prerequisites.

We end up in Twelve Steps because we deal with life by drinking and using. Take away the drugs and alcohol, and you have to actually deal with reality every waking moment. You need the tools and know-how. When using, the answers are simple. You're stressed? Get fucked up. Girlfriend left you? Go get fucked up. Bored? There's always getting fucked up. But once you stop drinking and using, you have to find ways to deal with life and its hardships. You have to deal with your emotions in healthier ways. You have to learn to live sober.

Many people didn't think I could do it. They didn't think I could stay sober. People around town had a betting pool on how long it would be before I started drinking again. I don't blame them for doubting me. Things were different now. What they didn't understand was that I had the *gift of desperation.* I was desperate to stay sober. I had about two months sober at this point, the longest I had gone without drinking since being a child, and it hadn't been easy. Those sober days were hard fought. I had no intention of restarting the clock.

With time, I learned how to relate to restaurant people again. Many people in the recovery community spend all of their time with each other. That wasn't an option for me. On a practical level, I worked nights. I was at work while other people were out socializing. People were either at work or asleep when I was free. In the early days, I spent a lot of time alone. I watched movies at home. I cooked for myself.

I was going to Twelve Steps meetings every day and did make good friends in the recovery community. This was good for my sobriety. I always had someone to call in moments of weakness. While this was an important support network, I did not want to abandon the service industry community. The restaurant community is close knit, especially in a small city like Charleston. Everyone knows each other. We are a family. This was my tribe, and I wasn't willing to abandon it just because I was sober now.

Staying connected to that community was hard at first. At the time, socializing was centered on alcohol—there was no getting around that. Most of my friends outside the recovery community were drinkers. We often had a harder time relating now. I went out with some of them after work one night and ordered a soda water. I wanted to be part of the group. It was awkward. They didn't know what to say. They felt like they couldn't talk about drinking. They didn't want to talk about my drinking problem, as many of them had drinking problems of their own that they weren't ready to acknowledge.

This got worse before it got better. I stopped getting invited to things as much. Some friends drifted away. This is a typical experience for the newly sober. Hank, the restaurant owner, had been sober for about a decade when he sent me to rehab. He warned me that early sobriety was going to be a lonely time. I have a richer life now, and it is easier to relate to people whether they drink or not, but I did lose friends. I did feel isolated.

There was nothing to do but accept these things. You have to let go of what was before you can get to where you're headed. It can be lonely in the meantime, but you will rebuild relationships and forge new ones. Today, it's not an issue for me, and I have a rich life, but those early days were rough. They were isolating. But I pushed through.

THE END OF A MARRIAGE

I was also dealing with the wreckage of my relationship. My wife was staying with a mutual friend in Philadelphia. She was waiting tables at a new job and getting certified as a personal trainer. We hadn't seen each other since she came to visit me in rehab. She had been very angry. She had every right to be. Being married to me must have been horrific. I put her through hell. She had left the Pavilion and gone back to Philly with the matter of our marriage and separation unresolved.

We talked on the phone after I got out and agreed to give each other some space. I was learning how to be sober at home and at work. When I wasn't at work, I was at meetings. I was trying to heal myself. I was learning how to live again. I didn't have the capacity to work on our marriage too. We agreed to revisit the matter in a few months.

I eventually flew out to Philadelphia to meet with her. We went to see a marriage counselor. She was still very angry. I understood that anger, but it brought me back to a bad place. Here we were, fighting again. It was the same toxic dynamic—I was the fuckup and she was the fixer. Everything was made out to be my fault, which wasn't a healthy dynamic to reenter. Not for me, and not for her.

That was when I accepted that we really weren't right for each other. We were already starting to move on. I was learning to live sober. I was the best I had been in decades. She was doing better too. When I first arrived, before the fighting started back up, she seemed lighter and more carefree than she had in years. She looked healthy and happy. She was back in school, pursuing a new passion. If everything really was my fault and she dropped everything and came back to Charleston only for it not to work out … well, that would be my fault too.

"We have to let each other go," I said. "You're in a good place. I'm in a good place."

She said okay. Though clearly upset, she didn't protest. She must have felt hurt that it was me making the final decision to end things. She had put up with my drinking, drug use, and crappy behavior for years. She had put up with the broken promises, the broken vows, the constant turmoil and chaos that surrounded me. Now I was finally getting my act together and getting sober, and suddenly I didn't want her anymore? That couldn't have felt good.

But I also knew in my heart that it was the right decision. I think she did too.

Things were amicable at first. We still talked on the phone. We tried to be supportive. Unfortunately, our relationship soured a few months later when she started dating someone new. Things got nasty around the divorce. She hired a divorce attorney to threaten me in court. It was a bad experience.

Sadly, we don't talk anymore. She eventually remarried and had kids. She moved on with her life, as I did with mine. She is the only one of my exes that I haven't stayed in touch with. I hope she's happy. I hope one day we can get together for coffee and reconcile as friends.

MAKING AMENDS AND GIVING BACK

There is probably no way to make it through recovery without leaving some people behind. Addiction leaves a trail of carnage in its wake. We do things we shouldn't. We hurt people we wish we hadn't. We make terrible choice after terrible choice. Making amends for those wrongs is a major part of the recovery process. Unfortunately, some wounds cannot be healed. My marriage was ultimately a casualty of my addiction.

But I still had to go through the process. In fact, I went through it formally *twice*, once in rehab and then again with Sheldon. He didn't care that I had already worked through the steps before he became my sponsor.

"I'm your sponsor. We're starting over," he said. "Are you willing to do what it takes or not?"

So I started from the top and went through the whole process again. It wasn't what I wanted, but it was definitely what I needed. The process was just as brutal the second time around. Delving back into my past was a gut-wrenching process that revealed just how much healing I still had to do.

Sheldon knew that recovery is a lifelong journey. I wasn't going to be working the steps twice—I was going to be working them *forever*. You don't just take a moral inventory of your wrongs, pass out apologies, and wash your hands of the past. We are constantly negotiating with the past. My anger and resentments ran deep. It was going to take me decades of introspection to work through them. It is a process I am still working through today.

The hardest part has always been reconciling my past with my mother. Even today, being in a room with my mother sometimes makes the hair on my neck stand on end. She hurt me so deeply, and I couldn't make sense of her reasoning. To be fair, I know I hurt her as well. Any reconciliation was hard, but I had to try. I called her that April for Easter to make amends. I apologized for many of the things that I had said and done.

But as with my marriage, this wasn't a one-sided conflict. My mother had injured me grievously. I couldn't understand the choices she had made. I had to give voice to that grief and resentment in order to move past them.

"I wish you wouldn't have abandoned me," I said. "I think that really sucks."

This was just the truth. Unfortunately, she wasn't ready to hear it at the time. She would eventually apologize, but not then. We kept talking, though. Things weren't perfect between us, but we were working toward something better than what we had. It was just going to take time. I was willing to put in the work if she was.

That was what Sheldon was trying to show me by starting over with the steps. He wasn't thumping the Big Book for no reason. He wanted me to understand that this was a process and that it would never end.

I am forever grateful for his wisdom and support. He was and is a mentor, a role model, and sometimes a disciplinarian. He was the father figure I hadn't had since my father and grandfather passed away. When Sheldon once put his hand on my shoulder and said that he was proud of me, I broke down and cried. It was like having a father again. He was teaching me how to be sober, which is more than just not drinking. He was teaching me to be a better man.

He was teaching me how to be sober, which is more than just not drinking. He was teaching me to be a better man.

I owe him my life. He would dismiss that notion and say that I had helped him and that he was only giving me what had been given to him. Maybe so, but that doesn't change the facts. He was under no obligation to help. He saved my life.

The beauty of the recovery community is that we take when we are sick and in need and we give back from a position of health and strength. We are all just lost souls trying to save each other. There is a sense of camaraderie in the recovery community. Someone is always there to offer a hand. Getting sober alone is hard, maybe impossible. Most need help. When we receive it, we then give back by paying it forward.

This isn't just the right thing to do—it's a crucial part of recovery. We cannot get sober without healing and learning to live as functioning members of society. That means being part of our communities and lifting each other up. As addicts, we have to watch out for each other. We have to give back.

After a year or two sober, it was my turn. Sheldon started cracking the whip. It was my turn to start sponsoring others. I didn't feel ready but was excited to start anyway. The recovery community had given me so much. Sheldon had given me so much. Hank, in an act of compassion, had given me so much. He didn't have to send me to rehab—he could have just fired me. Sheldon could have said no. No one had to help. But they did, and I owe my life to that fact. I wanted to repay the favor. I wanted to show others the same hope and kindness that had been shown to me.

I didn't know it yet, but that was the only way to stay sober. We were all addicts and alcoholics. The people walking into their first meeting and I were in the same boat, and we all needed to row together. It was the only way we were going to get anywhere.

Chapter 11

ON THE INDIGO ROAD

CORPORATE LIFE

2004–2009

Charleston, South Carolina, and Palm Coast, Florida

The longer I was sober, the better life got. The staff at Peninsula Grill regained faith in me. The owners started to trust me again. I felt more confident in my sobriety and more connected with my community. Life started to feel good for the first time in a long time. I was hopeful again.

Two years into sobriety, I started to think about where my career was headed next. Something inside was telling me it was time to move on. This was a startling revelation. So much of my life was wrapped up in the Peninsula Grill. I had helped create and open the restaurant. I got sober and restarted my life there. That kitchen, the bar, the dining room, the break room—my heart and soul were wrapped up in the structure and the people. It was all a part of me and always would be. But my passion for being there was gone.

I resigned shortly thereafter. I was conflicted about the choice. Hank had saved my life by sending me to rehab. I felt guilty about abandoning the store now. But I also longed for a new start without the burden of the history I had at the restaurant.

Putting in my resignation was an act of faith. Leaving was also scary in a material sense. I didn't have a job lined up, and the restaurant was still paying my rent as part of my compensation package. My savings were depleted after paying back more than $30,000 for rehab. I didn't know what was next, but it felt like time to move on. I wanted a life of purpose. I didn't know what that purpose was, but I wasn't going to find it by being so deeply unhappy at work.

I wasn't going to let fear of the unknown hold me back. My entire journey through sobriety was an act of faith. I had to have faith that the path I was on was the right one. I followed my heart and my intuition when choosing to view the intervention as my path. I had to have faith in my path to leave my marriage and to keep working at the Peninsula Grill after getting sober. Now my inner voice was telling me to move on and find purpose elsewhere. I wasn't going to ignore that voice. It had been my guiding light through recovery. I was again going to surrender myself to fate and trust that the universe would take care of me. This mentality had helped me get sober. Dismissing it now out of caution or fear would have been a mistake.

I left work and vacated my rental home. A friend from the recovery community put me up in their guest room while I figured out what came next. I started interviewing for jobs, most of which I didn't really want. A company offered me a six-figure salary to take a job in rural Florida. I turned it down because there wasn't an active Twelve Steps community in the area. I wasn't willing to put my sobriety at risk by being removed from the recovery community.

Fast forward a few months. My savings were gone. I was living on credit cards. There weren't any good offers coming through. I was starting to get desperate and anxious. I had a panic attack in bed one night. I couldn't sleep for worrying about what was going to happen. It was like I had reverted to that insecure kid who didn't have a home or a place to be. My faith was starting to feel shaky. I turned to God for reassurance. "God, I know you're going to take care of me," I said aloud, "but could you please do it now?" At this point, I was willing to go anywhere and do anything and trust in him that it would be okay.

"God, I know you're going to take care of me," I said aloud, "but could you please do it now?"

The very next day, the phone rang. People I had worked with at the Ritz-Carlton in St. Louis wanted me to interview with Ginn Resorts, where they now worked. They needed a food-and-beverage manager for a new golf resort. I drove to Florida for the interview, certain that the job was mine, not because of the personal connection but because God had once again answered my prayer.

I had not intended to go back into resorts, certainly not a golf resort. This was not what I had in mind when praying for a job, but this was the answer given. I put my trust in God and the universe and told myself that the path before me was the right one. I just had to be always searching my soul and adjusting course as needed. When they offered me the job, I accepted. In December, I packed my things and moved to Palm Coast, Florida.

Working in resorts was a nice change of pace after so many years in restaurants. This was a corporate job for a large multinational. It was very different from working in a tiny independently operated restaurant. I wore suits to work. I was in charge of a lot of people and teams. It was outside my comfort zone, but I felt up to the challenge.

Moving to Florida had the added benefit of giving me back some anonymity. Charleston is a small town, and the restaurant industry is insular. I was several years sober at this point, but people still thought of me as "the guy that had gone to rehab." Leaving town allowed me to hit the reset button. No one at the resort knew about my past. They could only judge me on my performance. I never talked about my past. I wanted to keep my personal and professional lives separate for a while.

I did well in the job. The resort was successful. Shortly after the grand opening, they promoted me to vice president of food and beverage. I moved to Orlando to be at the corporate office. This was not without growing pains. I was the youngest vice president at Ginn Resorts and very much the odd man out in a corporate environment.

Going to Orlando allowed me to reconnect with the recovery community. Palm Coast was a small town without much of a Twelve Steps presence. In Orlando, I found a group and started going to meetings. I forged new relationships there. I started to trust my sobriety more. I no longer felt dependent on the recovery community in Charleston. I was able to move around freely and find sober people anywhere. This felt like an inflection point in my journey through addiction. Things were getting easier and feeling more stable. The sense of impending doom that had hung over my entire life receded into the background.

My professional life was also feeling back on track. I was focusing on my career and learning so much. The Ginn organization operated a number of resorts, hotels, and private clubs. Before it was all said and done, I was overseeing eight properties and eight hundred employees. I helped design a $100 million hotel. I learned how to design and concept restaurants on a budget. These were skills that would later serve me well as an entrepreneur. My time spent working in a corporate environment prepared me for what came next.

THE ACCIDENTAL ENTREPRENEUR

2009–2013

I spent five good years with Ginn Resorts. The company was soaring—until suddenly it wasn't. The financial crisis and the collapse of the housing market hit the travel industry hard. The company started to stumble and sputter. Then came the layoffs. I was among them.

My next step wasn't clear to me. I didn't want to go back to Charleston or the restaurant business. I wanted to keep working in hotels and resorts. The corporate life had its perks. The pay was good. My nights were free. I wasn't ready to give all that up. Ginn Resorts issued me a severance package, which gave me time to look for the right job.

I was interviewing all across the country, mostly for jobs I wasn't very interested in. This was 2009, in the trough of the Great Recession, and good jobs weren't easy to come by. There was one job in Chicago that seemed like the right fit. I was going through a series of interviews with them, but it was taking time to close on an offer. They were hesitant to hire in such a bad economy.

During this time, I went on a hike in the highlands of North Carolina. The countryside was beautiful and put me into a meditative state. At one point, I was standing before a waterfall and reflecting on my career. I had a strong résumé. *Someone* was going to hire me eventually. But I didn't want just any job. I was about to turn forty. I had grown so much in the last few years. I was ready for work that would give me a real sense of purpose, not just a paycheck. It occurred to me that mentoring would give me that sense of purpose. I had always loved training people in restaurants. My mentors in the hospitality industry as well as the recovery community had given me so much. I wanted to give back by passing that knowledge and kindness forward. What higher calling could there be?

I was ready for work that would give me a real sense of purpose, not just a paycheck.

"I want to mentor," I said aloud. "I want to give back."

As if a prayer were being answered, my cell phone rang not fifteen minutes later. I could still hear the rush of the waterfall behind me. It was Kevin, an old friend in the industry. He told me to expect a call from a Michael Meyer, who owned a steakhouse in Charleston called Oak. They were in financial trouble and needed a consultant who could turn the restaurant around.

Working in a restaurant, in Charleston of all places, was definitely not part of my plan. But I always say the best way to make God laugh is to make a plan. My severance package was running out. The job in Chicago wasn't coming through. So I flew out to Charleston and met with Mike. I agreed to come on as a consultant for thirty days. It was a chance to make a little money while continuing to interview in Chicago. I was going to do my thirty days, help turn the restaurant around, and get on with my life.

Oak was a cool little steakhouse that was just going through hard times during the recession. I helped them implement more efficient systems that would cut costs and boost revenue. Three weeks into the consulting gig, I went to New York City to brief Mike and his partner, Andy O'Keefe, on our progress. They wasted no time declaring their real intentions.

"You're the most sane person we have talked to since the

restaurant opened," Mike said. It was the first thing out of his mouth. "We don't want you to leave. We want you to come on as a partner."

I was hesitant. The company was already losing money. They would be losing even more if they brought me on full time. I was honest with them about this fact. "If we're going to do this, we need to open more restaurants," I said, hoping to put them off the idea.

It didn't work. They said okay. We shook—and that was that. We were going to start a restaurant group and open a whole slate of properties.

There is no overstating how crazy this venture was at the time. We were in the middle of the worst recession in a century. Their only property was losing money, and it was a terrible time to be opening more. I had expected them to shrug off the idea. I was *hoping* they would say no. Running a business was not part of my plan. I still wanted the job in Chicago. I wanted reasonable hours and a steady income. My last entrepreneurial adventure had been a disaster, and that had been in a good economy.

Regardless, I didn't have anything else going on. Mike and Andy had so much faith in me that it proved too hard to say no and too hard to back out. There was a reason I hadn't turned them down. I had always wanted to own my own restaurants. Something told me that this was the right path. As before, I chose to follow my intuition and push aside my fears. I was going to walk this path. I started looking at properties that might make a good restaurant for our first joint venture.

At about this time, I got a call from the job in Chicago. They were ready to hire me. It felt like a cruel joke. I still wanted the job. I was still scared of going into business with Andy and Mike. Technically, we only had a handshake deal. In a legal sense, there was nothing stopping me from backing out on the deal and taking the safer route. But I remembered what Sheldon had taught me about having integrity, being a man of my word, and finishing what I started. I turned down the job in Chicago and went back to looking at properties.

My friend Bob Ulrich came up with the name for the company. We called it Indigo Road. When South Carolina was just a colony, indigo was the major cash crop. Charleston was one of the wealthiest cities in the colonies thanks to indigo. Bob pointed out that throughout my life, the road kept pointing back to Charleston. The name of the company honored both the place and my personal history. Further research revealed that the color indigo sometimes represented intuition. This seemed fitting given how my life had been shaped by my following the niggling voice in the back of my head. Call it intuition, call it faith, call it God, but that voice has been my guiding light through recovery and life.

I never planned to be an entrepreneur, but this was now my path, and I had to have faith that it was the right one. It was certainly not easy. We didn't make any money the first two years. We were still operating Oak at a loss. We launched a sushi restaurant called O-Ku.

O-Ku was partially the result of my deep love for Japanese cuisine and culture. One of my favorite words is *omotenashi*, which is Japanese and translates as "to wholeheartedly serve our guests," a sentiment we aspire to in all of our restaurants. While O-Ku would eventually go on to become one of our successful restaurants, things started slow. We had to have faith and keep doing the work while so many of the tables sat empty.

The slow business was largely a function of the bad economy, but I blamed myself. Mike and Andy had loaned me $750,000 to open O-Ku. I didn't have that kind of capital myself. I often stayed up late at night, having panic attacks about squandering their money. I kept questioning my decision to turn down the corporate job in

Chicago. I wondered if it had all been a big mistake.

In January of 2011, things started to turn around. The economy was in a slow recovery. We started seeing returns on quality improvement and more thoughtful hiring practices. Both restaurants were seeing more traffic. The numbers got a little better each month. We opened two new Charleston restaurants, the Macintosh in fall 2011 and the Cocktail Club in the summer. Both were in the black right out of the gate. The Macintosh was nominated as best new restaurant in America by both James Beard and *Bon Appétit*. In 2013, we opened Indaco, an Italian restaurant in Charleston. Again, it was a hit.

After three years of uncertainty and doubt, I felt confident in my life choices. It was a magical time, exhilarating and rewarding. We had gone from one failing concept to five successful restaurants over the course of four years. We were building a successful company, doing what we loved. It felt transformative and restorative. It was as if my personal curse had been lifted. I stopped worrying about the past and finally really believed in a better future.

PEOPLE-CENTERED, VALUES-DRIVEN BUSINESS

Two things make the Indigo Road what it is: our *people* and our *values*.

Restaurants are all about people. A great concept, a pretty building, the perfect menu—none of that means anything without the right people. Nothing can compensate for having the wrong staff. A good shift leader can transform the whole floor. I have watched sales tick up after replacing managers.

The right people are those who share our values. We look for people with a strong work ethic and collaborative spirit. They have to be passionate about the service industry and take pride in their work. Indifference is the enemy of hospitality. Our staff truly cares about the experiences they create for guests. Fine dining is all about creating an experience. They also have to be intellectually curious. Our concepts are high-end, cutting-edge restaurants. The staff is always learning in order to keep up.

We hold the same values at the executive level. We are passionate about the industry and always learning. We studied under the industry's heavy hitters, such as restaurateur Danny Meyer, and brought in consultants to design the best restaurants. There is working *in* your business, and there's working *on* your business. We are always looking for ways to make our restaurants better. We pass down what we learn about food, presentation, and service to everyone in the company.

I can teach you to chop a vegetable or ring up a check. I can teach you to take reservations and make cocktails. What *cannot* be taught, at least not quickly, are values and the personal qualities that we seek to hire. Intellectual curiosity, passion, a collaborative spirit—these aren't things I can impart over a week of training. This is why we hire based on values rather than technical skill. We don't always get it right, but when we do, our restaurants are better for it. You can see it in the numbers.

We owe everything to our employees. The Indigo Road simply wouldn't be possible without these amazing people. I am just one person. I run the company with a few other partners. Our nearly one thousand employees do the bulk of the work. Every night, they're out there on the floor, behind the bar, or in the kitchen, making it all happen. I need them a lot more than they need me. They are *more* important than our guests. Employee satisfaction is our number one priority.

I am so grateful to people like Danny Meyer, who was the first person to give this people-centered approach to hospitality a name and a voice. Author of *Setting the Table*, he literally wrote the book on internal hospitality. He has shown that happy staff makes for happy guests. Creating a positive experience for guests starts with creating a positive experience for your employees. When the staff feels good about the work they do, the food they serve, and the experience they create, the guests take note. That kind of burning passion is infectious. The staff serves the guests, and the company serves its employees.

This is just another way of saying that restaurants do best when operating from shared core values. You hire people that share your values. My values came from the recovery community. I learned so much from people like Sheldon. I am constantly repeating his words, not just in support groups but also in our restaurants. Integrity, honesty, hard work, radical transparency, the ability to admit and atone for mistakes, being open-minded and curious—these are things I learned in recovery. We apply them every day in the way we treat guests, in the way we treat each other. The principles of recovery are about learning how to live authentically, how to serve, and how to be a functioning member of the community. They help you run a better business as surely as they help you live a better life.

Our core values have allowed us to maintain quality as we grow. We now have over twenty restaurants operating across five states. In the world of high-end restaurants, growth is a double-edged sword. Growth means more revenue, but some patrons assume that quality goes down as the company grows. When we had the chance to replicate Oak in Atlanta in 2016, we were particularly worried that we would be viewed as a chain.

There is a kernel of truth to this bias. When we were smaller and only in Charleston, I was in every restaurant almost every night of the week, visiting tables and checking in with staff. I knew all the regulars and every single employee by name. I was so familiar with the restaurants that I could have covered almost anyone's shift. None of this is possible anymore. I feared that we would lose the personal connection with our employees and guests that had allowed us to create amazing experiences. The company has always felt like family, and I didn't want to lose that feeling.

For the most part, we have managed to maintain the company culture by sticking to our core values. I attend orientation for new employees each month in every restaurant. We talk about the company values, not just the basics of the job description. I give out my personal cell phone number. They are allowed to call me at any time, day or night, if they have a concern. We may be a bigger company, but we still care about employees, and we want them to feel like family. I'm not naive—that's a tall order. But we work very hard to make it a reality. That's been the key to our success.

THE BUSINESS OF GIVING BACK

Perhaps the most important part of recovery is giving back. This is one of our company values—perhaps the most important one. Indigo Road has allowed us to give back to the industry by creating better jobs. We prioritize employees and their happiness. This isn't just good for the bottom line—it's also good for the industry and its people. We'd like our jobs to be among the best someone ever has.

Indigo Road isn't just about money. We are a business. We have to make money to keep the lights on. But there are lots of ways to make money. What really brings me happiness is building better lives for our employees and a better community for our guests. We do this by treating employees with respect and kindness. Fine dining pays more than other segments of the restaurant industry. High-end food comes with bigger bills that mean higher tips. We have lots of people in management and the executive tier making six figures, and we promote from within.

We want employees to find meaning in their work. The industry has always been more than a job for me. It was my calling. I found a sense of purpose and community in hospitality. I am profoundly grateful to be in a position to offer the same thing to so many people. Employees who share our values are inherently satisfied with their work. They care about what they are doing and find it just as rewarding as we do.

Showing your employees kindness and respect celebrates human dignity. We want our employees to feel loved, and appreciated. Creating a better working environment for our people has been one of the great accomplishments of my life. We want them to find financial, emotional, and spiritual success. We are always looking for ways to make their lives better.

We recently established a loan program to help employees cover the down payment on a new home. I overheard one of our servers talking about wanting to buy a home. They could afford mortgage payments, which weren't any higher than their rent, but they didn't have the money for a down payment. It occurred to me that the company did have the capital and liquidity. We established an interest-free loan program to help employees buy homes. They pay back the loan on an installment basis over the course of three years. Many of our employees are now homeowners thanks to the program.

Indigo Road also gives back to the wider community. Each year, we work with or support up to a hundred charities. We partner with nonprofits to deliver food to the homeless and hungry. Featuring local chefs, we hold fund-raisers that can raise half a million dollars in a night. We donate to local soup kitchens and community pantries. We work with shelters, such as City of Refuge in Atlanta, that help addicts and trafficking victims get back on their feet. Each year, we support over a hundred charities on average.

Much of our charity focuses on hunger in the community and addiction within the industry. These are causes that matter to me as a recovering addict and formerly homeless youth. We encourage employees to use the company to pursue their causes as well. We ask about the charities and causes that matter to them and look for ways to help. Homelessness and addiction are my pet issues and, as philanthropic causes, are a natural fit for Indigo Road. The food-and-beverage industry is uniquely positioned to help with hunger and homelessness. Addiction is such a problem in the industry that addressing it is foundational to caring for our own. But our people care about lots of causes, and we are always looking for more ways to help them give back in ways that are meaningful to them.

Indigo Road is proof that a successful business can do more than make money—it can also make an impact. The company feels like another answered prayer. I will always remember standing at that waterfall and praying for a job with meaning and impact and not fifteen minutes later getting the phone call that would lead me down this road. I thank God for that call. And I thank

It's the privilege of my life to work alongside them as we build better lives, a better industry, and a stronger community.

God for the restaurant industry and its people. I wouldn't be here without them, and it's the privilege of my life to work alongside them as we build better lives, a better industry, and a stronger community.

I will never have the words to fully express my gratitude to the women and men, past and present, of the Indigo Road. They inspire me not only to be a better leader but also a better person.

To the Indigo Road family, it is my daily prayer that I would be deserving of your respect. From the bottom of my heart, thank you.

Chapter 12

BEN'S FRIENDS

THE SECRET LIFE OF BEN MURRAY

Summer 2017

Florence, South Carolina

While eating breakfast with Mickey Bakst, one of my best friends, the subject of addiction in the hospitality industry came up. Mickey was thirty or forty years sober and also part of the recovery community. We both agreed it was ironic that people in an industry steeped in alcohol and drugs had such a problem getting help with addiction. This is part of the duality of the industry that I mentioned earlier. The industry normalizes alcohol and drugs so much that addicts easily go unnoticed or unacknowledged in our ranks. They don't get help because no one takes their problems seriously. They have trouble finding each other despite so many people in the industry struggling with the same problems.

We both agreed that the restaurant business needed an industry-specific meet-up group for people who are sober or trying to get sober. Major cities have many Twelve Steps groups, but these can be intimidating to people not already in the recovery community. The industry tells even very heavy drinkers that they don't have a problem. The stigma around addiction keeps people from seeking support. Industry people needed a place where they could talk about these issues with their peers.

Mickey and I talked about starting just such a group. Unfortunately, we were both busy, and it didn't materialize. We were incredibly busy. Indigo Road was growing rapidly. I was opening several restaurants. The idea got relegated to the back burner.

One of those restaurants was Town Hall, a farm-to-table Southern cuisine concept in Florence, South Carolina. The grand opening was set for later that summer, and we were short staffed. We really needed chefs. A prominent chef in Atlanta, Gena Berry, mentioned that Ben Murray was taking on short-term gigs and might be a good fit. I knew him. We'd met while opening Canoe together back in 1995. He later followed David and me to Savannah to open the restaurant that never materialized.

Ben had been a heavy partier back in the day. He drank. He took drugs. But he was also a good guy and a great chef. He had worked at Jean-Georges in Manhattan and for Wolfgang Puck out west. Gena had worked big food festivals with him. Ben was very experienced and loved by all.

I gave him a call and asked if he would help open the restaurant. We agreed on a salary and a start date, and the company put him up in a hotel in Florence. He showed up at the restaurant looking exactly the same as he had ten years earlier. This was a surprise. Drugs and alcohol can really age you. But Ben looked happy and healthy. He claimed to have cleaned up his act. In the restaurant business, that can mean anything from complete sobriety to just swapping hard drugs for alcohol and pot. I didn't pry. He was upbeat and enthusiastic. For six weeks, he worked every day from morning to midnight. He did a great job. I never once saw him take a drink.

After the restaurant opened on solid footing, I stopped spending as much time in Florence. Ben had done such a great job opening the restaurant that we were talking about inviting him to stay on permanently. We didn't want to let him go when his contract was up. Then, a few weeks later, I got a call from another one of the chefs at Town Hall.

"Hey, I'm worried about Ben," he said. "Something is up. He was a couple hours late to work the other day. Then yesterday he walked off in the middle of his shift, saying he had to go without saying why."

This came as a surprise. It didn't sound like Ben. I texted him to see what was going on and asked if we could chat. He said sure. I texted him back that I would come up the next day. He said okay.

The next morning, I drove the two hours from Charleston to Florence. My phone kept buzzing the whole time. Ben was sending anxious texts. He said there was no reason to come. He said he already knew he had blown it. I kept trying to call him from the road, but he wouldn't pick up. I had to keep pulling over to write back. I told him he hasn't blown anything. *I'm just coming to talk to you*, I kept writing. *You haven't blown anything, man. Pick up the phone.*

Nothing seemed to register. He wouldn't pick up. His texts became increasingly erratic. *Don't come*, he kept saying. *There's nothing to talk about.* This made me think that he was on a bender and didn't want me to see him drunk or hungover.

When I got to the hotel, he wouldn't come down to meet with

me. He stopped responding to texts. His car was in the parking lot, so I knew he was in his room. I just didn't know the room number. I considered asking the concierge desk for his room number, but I didn't want to make a scene. We did a lot of business with the hotel. The owner was a nice guy, and I didn't want to bother him or embarrass Ben.

At a loss, I called my girlfriend to get her opinion. "I don't know what to do. I'm a little worried. He's being really weird."

"Maybe you should call the police?" she said.

This seemed extreme. I said, "He's probably just on a bender and doesn't want me to see him shitfaced. I bet he passed out. I can catch up with him tomorrow when he can actually hold a conversation."

> *I texted Ben one more time before leaving. **Man, I just wish you would reach out to me.** No response.*

I texted Ben one more time before leaving. *Man, I just wish you would reach out to me.* No response.

I drove back to Charleston, sure we would work things out. We weren't going to fire him. He had done a great job the first six weeks. At Indigo Road, we care about our people. Those are our values. We don't toss people aside when they are having a hard time. If he was struggling with alcohol again, we were going to get him the help he needed.

In the years since, I have thought a lot about the decision to leave the hotel. I turn it over in my head. The temptation is to blame myself. Why didn't I call the police? Why didn't I get the room number from the hotel manager? Why didn't I do more? I try not to be too hard on myself. I would never blame another person for what happened next.

Friday evening, I got a call from the hotel owner, the very person I hadn't wanted to trouble. I'll never forget the flat tone of his voice, as if the life had been sucked out of him. "We just rushed Ben Murray to the hospital."

"What do you mean?" I said, not comprehending.

Someone had reported the sound of a gun going off at the hotel. The staff found Ben in his room with a gunshot wound to the head.

"Steve," he said solemnly. "He's still alive."

I was in Greenville, South Carolina, at the time. I sprinted to my car and drove straight to Florence. When I got to the hospital, I tried to get information from the receptionists at the front desk. They couldn't tell me anything. I wasn't family. It would have been a HIPAA violation to divulge medical information to me. I pleaded with them. But there was nothing they could do.

I wasn't about to leave, not this time. I paced the waiting room, not knowing what to do. A nurse saw me stumbling around in tears and stopped to talk. I begged her to tell me something—anything.

"Listen, I just want to talk to somebody," I said, still sobbing.

The nurse went into the back. After a while, another nurse came to find me. She was also tearing up. "Ben was here, but he's not here anymore," she said. Nothing more. That was all she would say, but it was enough.

I collapsed down into a chair, shell shocked, until finally it hit me—and utter despair sunk in. My mind flashed back to last weekend, when I was standing in the hotel parking lot by Ben's car, wondering if I should call the police or go inside. It was all I could think of—that and Ben, now gone.

Never in a million years would I have thought Ben capable of what he'd done. I had only ever known him as a happy person. His life seemed good. He loved cooking and playing blues guitar. He

141

loved people. He was always the life of the party. When he wasn't cracking a joke, he was laughing at someone else's. There had been no indication that he was depressed. Everyone thought he was doing a great job until that last week or two. His suicide just seemed so out of the blue. It made no sense.

The hospital staff told me that the family had been notified. I called Ben's mother on my way back home. We had never met, but I wanted her to know that someone was there for her and cared. She was in her eighties. Ben didn't have a lot of living family. I didn't want her to go through this alone.

It was a hard call to make. The pain in her voice was heartrending. We were both sobbing. We talked for a long time. The secret story of Ben's other life began to unfold. She told me that he had been trying to get sober for years. He had been in and out of detox six times. I knew he had been a drinker but nothing about this struggle.

This was by design. Ben hadn't wanted people to know. He feared the stigma of being an alcoholic. His mom wanted him to go to Twelve Steps meetings after getting out of rehab. Ben refused. He didn't want anyone to know he was struggling. He would say, "Mom, I'm better now. See?" But every time, he would go on another bender a few months later, and the cycle would repeat.

This was probably all exacerbated by mental health issues. His girlfriend later told me that he had been diagnosed with bipolar disorder. His mood could swing wildly. One day he could be the happy-go-lucky Ben we all knew and loved; the next, he would fall into a deep depression. This shed new light on the erratic text messages he had sent me. I had assumed he was on a bender. Maybe he was, but he was also having a mental breakdown. He wasn't well, but he was too ashamed of stigma to get help.

A DEADLY CODE OF SILENCE

Ben isn't here today because he didn't get help. Ben isn't here today because no one knew he *needed* help. No one knew what was going on with him. No one knew to reach out. He kept everything bottled up and hidden. We really had no idea. I had never once seen him take a drink at the restaurant. The hotel staff later told me that he would come back to the hotel around midnight, and drink alone at the bar for hours. He didn't want anyone at work knowing how he was drinking.

The terrible irony is that on opening night of the restaurant, there were at least four other people in the restaurant in active recovery. Three of them were chefs working alongside Ben. He would have known this too. He also knew that Mickey and I were sober and in recovery. Still, he never reached out for help.

I cannot speak for Ben. Maybe he just didn't want our help. Maybe he wanted to keep drinking and didn't want us intervening. What I *do* know is that there is something about the industry that keeps people from getting the help they need.

For too long, our industry has obeyed a dangerous code of silence. The industry normalizes drinking and using drugs as a way to deal with the stress of working in the industry. The code prevents us from questioning a coworker's relationship to alcohol and drugs. You aren't allowed to question someone's drinking. Offering help makes assumptions that aren't allowed. I am happy to say that, slowly, this is finally changing.

> *For too long, our industry has obeyed a dangerous code of silence.*

Addiction is overwhelmingly common in the industry. Study

after study bears this out. The Substance Abuse and Mental Health Services aggregated study data from 2008 to 2012 showed that 17.5 percent of food preparation and service industry workers were heavily abusing alcohol, a higher rate than was seen in any other industry.[1] They also reported that 19.1 percent of food preparation and service industry workers had engaged in recent illicit drug use, also the highest of any job category. We are literally killing ourselves with alcohol and drugs.

Up until now, few wanted to speak out. No one wants to ask the other people on the floor, behind the bar, or in the kitchen whether they have a problem. Even the heaviest drinking and drugging gets rationalized away. We see a coworker blacking out at the bar again, and we say, "He just likes to party." We let him "sleep it off." Maybe we get him a cab, but we don't ask questions. We don't voice concern. People doing cocaine or meth in the break room are just "looking for a little boost to get through the shift." Drinking every night is normal. "They're just blowing off steam." No one ever has a problem—not a real *problem*; they're just partying. It's all okay.

It's not okay. These are the same things people said about me. I was drinking heavily and taking drugs at work for years. No one said anything until it finally started to affect my work. I was taking shots at the bar and doing cocaine in the walk-in freezer, and it was no secret. Everyone thought I was good because I was still getting the job done. I was getting praise. I was getting promoted. How could I have a problem?

The industry code says that you can get as messed up as you want as long as you get your ass in to work the next day and do the job.

---

1   Donna M. Bush and Rachel N. Lipari, "Substance Use and Substance Use Disorder by Industry," SAMHSA, April 16, 2015, https://www.samhsa.gov/data/sites/default/files/report_1959/ShortReport-1959.html.

You can get high at work as long as you take care of the guests. That's the code. Getting trashed is part of the lifestyle. It doesn't matter how much you are drinking or what drugs you are taking—as long as you can do the job, everyone will say you are good.

But we aren't always good. Otherwise, service industry workers wouldn't have higher rates of alcohol and drug abuse than those in any other industry. We also wouldn't have such abysmally high rates of mental health issues. The nonprofit Mental Health America released a 2017 study[2] showing that work environment in the food-and-beverage industry was correlated with high levels of mental health issues. A 2018 study[3] in the *American Journal of Epidemiology* showed that tipped workers were at higher risk of depression than nontipped workers.

In my opinion, the mental health crisis in the industry is a function of our problem with addiction. We drink too much. People say the job is stressful. A lot of jobs are stressful. When I hear someone saying they can't handle the stress, I wonder how they are dealing with that stress. Drugs and alcohol are the industry's favorite coping mechanisms, but they only make matters worse.

The problem is that we are all complicit. We let our own people slip deep into addiction before they ever get any help. We let them slip into despair, and we say nothing. No one notices until these people start missing shifts or getting too drunk at work. No one notices until they get locked up. No one notices until they die in a

---

2   Michele Hellebuyck, et al., "Mind the Workplace," MHA, 2017, https://www. mentalhealthamerica.net/sites/default/files/Mind%20the%20Workplace%20 -%20MHA%20Workplace%20Health%20Survey%202017%20FINAL.pdf.

3   Tracy Brawley and John Kirkland, "The Tipping Point: Service Sector Employees Are More Susceptible to Mental Health Issues," Oregon Health and Science University, July 31, 2018, https://news.ohsu.edu/2018/07/31/the-tipping-point-service-sector-employees-are-more-susceptible-to-mental-health-issues.

car accident or in the bathroom with a needle in their arm.

We have to break the code of silence and start taking care of each other. We take care of other people every night. That's the job. We are a community literally dedicated to service. It's time we start taking care of each other.

The hospitality industry is incredibly giving. We form charities. We work in soup kitchens. We throw fund-raisers. We serve the community every single day and night. We care for others. We serve guests, but we don't serve each other. We give back to the community while abandoning our own.

The great lie is that everyone makes it. They don't all make it. Ben didn't make it. Every year, people are getting diagnosed with cirrhosis. They're falling out from overdoses. They're committing suicide. They are crashing cars and getting arrested and losing families and jobs. They are getting addicted. They are losing everything, including their lives.

We see these things every day in our communities and places of work, and we do nothing. In fact, we do *worse* than nothing. We actively support each other's addictions. We give each other cover. We make excuses for everyone's bad behavior. We support each other in our addictions.

This only makes a toxic environment more toxic. Our industry is awash in drugs and alcohol. When I was using, it felt impossible to be in the industry and be sober. The industry is all I loved and knew. It was all anyone would pay me for. Leaving felt impossible. Staying in the industry and being sober felt implausible. I was at a complete loss until people finally stepped in to get me the help that I needed.

Maybe that's how Ben felt. Maybe he thought sobriety wasn't possible. I can only speculate. He didn't get the help I did, and now he isn't here to say.

BEN'S FRIENDS

November 2016–present

Ben's death saddled me with an enormous burden of guilt. If only I had stepped in … if only I had done something … if only I had tried harder to get into that hotel room … if only I had forced my way in. These hypotheticals turned over and over in my head. It was too late to save Ben, but there were many more people in our industry living on the edge. I wanted to do something that would keep them alive.

Shortly after Ben's suicide, I met with Mickey for breakfast again. We talked about Ben. We talked about addiction and how it was ravaging our industry.

"Remember that support group we wanted to start?" I asked him. "I'm going to do this."

"I'm going to do it with you," he said.

This time, we didn't delay. People were dying, and it was incumbent on all of us in the industry to do something now. This was going to be our best attempt.

We called the group Ben's Friends. We held the first meeting at one of our Charleston restaurants in November of that year. The meetings were a safe space for industry people to come

> *People were dying, and it was incumbent on all of us in the industry to do something now.*

together and talk about addiction and sober living. We were industry people talking to industry people. We speak the same language. We can speak to the specifics of addiction in the industry and understand what other industry people go through. We all understand how ubiquitous alcohol is in the industry. We understand how isolating it can be to pass on going to the bar with coworkers after your shift.

147

This creates a sense of belonging that makes people more likely to reach out for the help they need to get sober. People come together to share stories and ask questions. They engage in free-form discussion around a general topic. Everyone is allowed to interject and comment. We want to encourage people to build community with other sober people so that they can build out a support network.

About a dozen people showed up to the first meeting. Word spread quickly, and each week there were more new faces. We had hit on a real need. New chapters started popping up. An industry veteran in Atlanta read an article about the group and wanted to start one in their city. Scott Crawford, one of the sober chefs who worked at Town Hall beside Ben, started a chapter in Raleigh. Gabe Rucker, a chef who owns and operates the French-cuisine restaurant Le Pigeon, after getting a cold call from Mickey, agreed to start a chapter in Portland. As of fall 2019, we are now in seven cities, spanning from coast to coast and expanding all the time. Every day more people are reaching out and wanting to start a chapter in their city. It is truly inspiring. The camaraderie and sense of community and safety that I see in the eyes of these meetings' attendees brings me to tears regularly. The same community that accepted my drug and alcohol abuse is now leaning in to help each other in a way that is profound.

The media has been instrumental in getting the word out. Ben's Friends was getting positive coverage in print media and on air.

Historically, the media has contributed to the glorification of drugs and alcohol in the industry. Reality TV codified the image of the "bad boy" celebrity chef living the rock 'n' roll lifestyle. These stereotypes get clicks and eyeballs, but they also perpetuate a fantasy. They give alcoholism and addiction a sexy makeover. Thankfully, the media has become more responsible in its coverage. When Anthony Bourdain committed suicide, a lot of people woke up to the dark side of the celebrity chef rock 'n' roll lifestyle. Bourdain was the quintessential "bad boy" celebrity chef—and now he's dead.

For so long, the media was silent on the problems in the industry. During the 2015 Charleston Wine and Food Festival, three chefs under the age of thirty-five died of heroin overdoses. The festival received massive coverage in local media. The overdoses were barely mentioned, if at all.

Thankfully, the cultural conversation is shifting—and not just in the media. The industry is finally starting to acknowledge its problems. The success of Ben's Friends speaks to that change. So does the existence of other organizations and outlets. Kat Kinsman, a senior editor of *Food & Wine* magazine, created a website called Chefs With Issues to help industry people deal with stress and personal problems in healthy ways. The conversation is changing the cultural narratives about the industry, too. Twenty years ago, it was a given that industry people drank heavily and took drugs. The industry was seen as a holding ground for college students and people who hadn't figured out their lives yet. Now that the industry has matured and more people are pursuing careers in hospitality, especially fine dining, we don't assume that people will float in and out of the industry.

When people stick around in the industry, we are forced to face their problems. If we want to keep people in the industry and see restaurants thrive, we are going to have to keep them healthy and alive.

At Ben's Friends, we are attempting to accelerate these changes in the cultural conversation. Twelve Steps programs place a premium on confidentiality and anonymity. They don't usually engage with the public. At Ben's Friends, we respect the privacy of our members, but one of our goals is to shine a light on the problem of addiction in the industry. We want to get people talking so that they will take action. This is the only way we will effect true change. We cannot save every person at Ben's Friends. We want to empower the whole industry to take care of its own.

Ben's Friends is not a one-stop recovery shop. It can't be. Most groups meet only once a week. No one walks into a Ben's Friends meeting and walks out sober for life. No one with a serious addiction overcomes it with an hour of group each week. That isn't realistic, and it isn't the goal. Recovery is a lifelong process. Ben's Friends is an *introduction* to recovery and the recovery community. We want to introduce people to recovery concepts in a familiar and welcoming environment and connect them to other resources and support. We operate in cities with lots of resources available to people who want to get sober, including daily support groups, addiction counselors, and rehabs.

The problem is that many people in the industry don't know how to access these resources. Many don't even know they exist. Others are just too scared to seek help. They find it easier to ignore their problems. We want to end the stigma. We want to *break the silence*. We are talking about addiction and sober living openly so that industry people can identify problems and know where to look for solutions.

A disheveled girl showed up to a Ben's Friends meeting a few years ago with dark circles under her eyes and a cloud over her head. She barely spoke at the meeting. She just listened. After the meeting, we gave her some information on support groups with more women. (We now have more women at meetings, but at the time it was mostly men.) She showed up at the restaurant a year later looking completely transformed. Her smile was beaming. Her face and skin had softened. Mickey and I barely recognized her when she came up to say that Ben's Friends had helped her get the support she needed to get sober. Mickey and I both had tears in our eyes. Here was walking, talking proof that our project was working and transforming lives.

We have watched Ben's Friends save our own employees. One of our employees was hooked on heroin and couldn't get clean because his roommate was also his heroin dealer. He came to the chef for help and was pointed to Ben's Friends. His living situation was unsafe. We raised the funds to send him to a sober-living home for a month. He's been clean two years now. We are now looking for creative ways to raise funds and grants to help people get out of dangerous situations and into safe housing. We hope to someday open sober-living communities and halfway houses for industry people.

These success stories prove two things: First, that there is a need for groups like Ben's Friends. People are showing up because they need help. Second, that the hospitality community cares about its own.

The code of silence around these issues is not an inherent part of industry culture. It's at odds with our values, a contradiction that we can address. We can create an industry culture in which it is okay to ask for help.

> *We can create an industry culture in which it is okay to ask for help.*

Ben's Friends will be the most important thing that I ever do, more important than my own company. With Indigo Road, we created a company based around the values and principles of recovery. With Ben's Friends, we are bringing those values to the greater hospitality industry. We are creating a better community within the wider industry. Ben's Friends is helping people save their lives. There's nothing more important to me on this journey—nothing.

Chapter 13

TOWARD A BETTER LIFE AND A STRONGER INDUSTRY

Ben's Friends is the culmination of my personal story. I owe my life to two things: the hospitality industry and the recovery community. My sense of identity is wrapped up in the restaurant business. The industry accepted me when nothing and no one else would. I found my sense of purpose and belonging in the industry. I nearly lost it all to addiction. My intervention was a second chance. Sobriety was a second chance. It's a gift. Recovery rates are abysmally low. Most people never really get sober, and fewer still remain that way for life.

I see myself in the people who come to Ben's Friends meetings. They remind me of that scared boy who needed love and support. They remind me of the teenager who thought himself broken and cursed. They remind me of the young man who had lost all hope and didn't believe that things could be better. To see these broken people come to their first Ben's Friends meeting, find their tribe, and start to heal is powerful. It's humbling and awe inspiring. And to know that my pain, traumas, and struggle are being channeled into helping other people heal is profound.

Mickey feels the same. Everyone working on Ben's Friends does too. We are all industry people who got sober and want to help others do the same. This is our community, and we are trying to lift it up. Scott once said that he wanted to leave the industry better than he'd found it. That resonated with me. The industry has given me so much. I want the industry to thrive and prosper. We can't keep losing people to overdoses, to burnout, to alcoholism, to suicide.

When you see someone in pain or struggling, don't do what I did with Ben. Do what we do at Ben's Friends. Be present. Be supportive. Reach out when something seems wrong. Be there for your people.

If you are struggling, know that you can be sober and that you can be happy. Don't be afraid to reach out for help. Don't be ashamed of addiction or depression. We have to break the stigma—lives depend on it. It's time to normalize recovery. Finding support has never been more possible. There are people who know what you are going through and want to help. You can find them. I found them. You can get sober.

But first you have to be honest with yourself. Addiction is the only disease that convinces people they are perfectly healthy. Cancer patients aren't walking around saying they don't have cancer. Admit your problem to yourself. Then tell someone who can help.

A better life is possible. As an alcoholic, I couldn't have even imagined my current life. Life now feels like a gift to be cherished and protected. I call it a gift because I literally asked for this life. I prayed for an intervention, and it happened. I trusted in God and walked forward in faith. I put in the work and became a man of integrity. I kept promises to others and to myself, and today my life has improved in profound ways. My relationships are varied and rich. I am closer to my sister and her son than I have ever been. My company has become successful beyond anything I could have imagined, and that money is supporting a thousand good jobs. Our nonprofit is saving lives.

I am now in the most functional relationship of my life with a woman whom I just married, Shelby, and our love is based on radical acceptance. My whole life has been in the pursuit of acceptance, often in unhealthy ways. There is nothing unhealthy about our relationship. She accepts me despite my baggage and scars. I do the same for her. We are raising her daughter, Madison, and I thank God for her every day. Through healing in sobriety and walking through life with faith, I am able to walk down paths that never seemed imaginable before.

Despite my best attempts at atonement, my addiction left a path of destruction in my wake. My ex-wife still won't talk to me. The wounds addicts inflict upon loved ones don't disappear when we get sober. Family can always be difficult in recovery, but in my case, I also had to come to terms with the scars my mother left on me. To get sober, I had to come to peace with how she treated me as a child.

Much soul-searching has allowed me to see her more sympathetically. She probably tried the best she could. I'm sure she had demons of her own. I know that she regrets many of her choices. She used to bring up my childhood constantly. She was always apologizing, even after I had formally forgiven her for abandoning me as a traumatized and sick child.

I had to ask her to stop bringing up the past. She had regrets that I could not make right for her. That is her journey. I forgave her, but that doesn't mean we are one big, happy family. We lost twenty long years. There is no getting them back. There is no erasing them, either.

She had regrets that I could not make right for her. That is her journey.

Part of living authentically is accepting things as they are. We won't ever be the Brady Bunch. We won't be gathering around the Christmas tree every year. My relationship with my mother will never be close, and things will always feel strained. I have made peace with that. We can meet for dinner sometimes. We can be nice and pleasant. It's not perfect, but it's more than we ever had before. I love my mother, and I am grateful for what we do have now.

My life is good and impossibly rewarding. I do not take it for granted. Owing my life to sobriety means that I could lose everything at any moment. Everything good in my life will disappear if I start to drink again. I have seen people sober for decades go back to drink and lose everything—their home, spouse, career, kids, everything. You can put the disease in remission by not taking that drink, by not popping that pill, but it never goes away.

Old-timers in the recovery community are known to claim that they are no further from drinking than the day they quit. The only defense is constant and permanent vigilance. As Sheldon would say, "Your disease is right outside the door doing push-ups, just waiting on you." I haven't had a drink in almost eighteen years. I was lucky to make it out alive last time. There is no guarantee I would survive another go-round.

People can easily forget this the longer they are sober precisely because they reap the benefits of sobriety. They forget how dark things used to be. Sheldon used to say, "Sometimes the hardest thing for an alcoholic is when everything goes right." You forget about the chaos, the DUIs, the wrecked cars, the lost jobs, the broken marriages. When life is good, it can be easy to think that it would be even better with a drink.

None of my greatest accomplishments—not the Indigo Road, not Ben's Friends, not any of the other philanthropic work we do—would have been possible without my sobriety. I owe it to good people in the hospitality industry and the recovery community. I hope to be paying back that debt for the rest of my life.

It's a huge debt. The restaurant business saved my life twice. The first time was in my early twenties, when I found unconditional love and acceptance in the industry at a time when I needed that more than anything. The second time came when I was thirty-two and two brave men cared enough about me to stage an intervention. There are no words that can fully capture the gratitude that I have for the hospitality industry and its wonderful people. I would simply not be here writing this without them. I would be dead. Instead, I am alive and forever in awe that these people were able to love me when I couldn't love myself.

ACKNOWLEDGMENTS

There are so many people to thank I couldn't possibly fit them all in, but I wanted to express my gratitude to the following people who have shaped my life and brought me to this moment:

To my amazing wife, Shelby, and my daughter, Madison: I wake up every day wanting to be a better version of myself for you, and to be a husband and father you can be proud of.

The women and men of the Indigo Road: night after night, you exude what it truly means to be hospitable. I strive daily to be the leader you deserve.

To my partners, Andy O'Keefe and Michael Meyer: thank you for your unwavering belief in me and this project.

To the Ferguson Family and Jane Eudy.

To Sheldon Weinstein: you are the most significant male figure I have ever had in my life. Thank you for teaching me how to walk the path of sobriety and how to be a man of my word.

To Mickey Bakst, the cofounder of Ben's Friends: thank you for leaning in and helping start a conversation about addiction in our industry. None of this would be happening without you.

To Scott Crawford and the many other chairs of Ben's Friends across the country: thank you for carrying an important message to the sick and suffering members of the restaurant family who need to know there is a different way to live.

To John T. Edge: thank you for encouraging me, celebrating diversity, and continuing to provide hope for a better South.

To Kat Kinsman: thank you for bringing humanity and compassion to the conversation surrounding the mental health challenges of our industry.

To Hunter Lewis and the team at *Food & Wine*: you are helping to spread the message of what it means to be an industry professional. Please accept my heartfelt thank you for your hard work telling the stories that need to be told.

To Darcy Shankland at *Charleston Magazine*: you asked me to write an article, and I wrote something completely different. Thank you for publishing it anyway—look what happened!

To Mary Reynolds: thank you for making me look good, which I know is a full-time job.

To the dozens of others who have played a pivotal role in my journey: please know that I am grateful for you and appreciate your continued support.

ABOUT THE AUTHOR

Steve Palmer is the managing partner and founder of the Indigo Road Hospitality Group. He formerly served as vice president of food and beverage for Ginn Clubs and Resorts and has worked in the hospitality industry in various capacities since the age of thirteen.

Palmer has been recognized by the *New York Times*, *L.A. Times*, NPR, *Southern Living*, *Food & Wine*, and Forbes Small Giants for his growing presence in the hospitality industry, as well as for his charitable and community efforts. In 2016, Palmer cofounded Ben's Friends, the food-and-beverage industry support group offering hope, fellowship, and a path forward to industry professionals struggling with substance abuse and addiction. He has presented on addiction in the industry at TEDx Charleston and various culinary events, among other venues.

MORE FROM STEVE

That's my story. What's yours? If you're in the industry and trying to get or stay sober, I urge you to reach out to someone. People want to help. If there's a Ben's Friends chapter in your town, think about attending to find or offer support. If there's not, there should be, and if you're interested in helping found one, we want to hear from you.

To reach out or learn more, visit **bensfriendshope.com**. Whoever you are, I hope you too find grace, hospitality, community, and happiness in life. God bless.